©Master Key
to the GRE

Volume 3

Word
Problems

Made by
Sherpa Prep

Master Key to the GRE: Word Problems.

ISBN: 978-0-9966225-3-0

Register Your Book!

To access the online videos that come with this book, please go to:

www.SherpaPrep.com/Activate

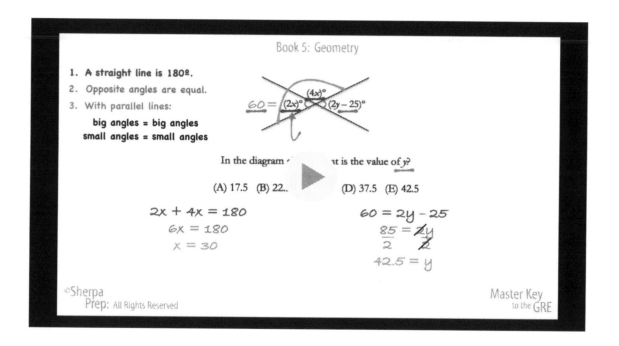

When registering:

Be sure to provide the **same** last name and shipping address that you used to purchase this book or to enroll in your GRE course with Sherpa Prep!

Register @ www.SherpaPrep.com/Activate

Master Key by
Sherpa Prep

Dear Student,

Thank you for purchasing Sherpa Prep's guide to <u>Word Problems</u>. We know that preparing for the GRE can be a grueling and intimidating process. The fact that you've chosen us to assist you is deeply appreciated.

This series of books is the culmination of nearly three decades of experience teaching the GRE on a daily basis. We think you'll find that experience and expertise reflected in the pages that follow.

As with any undertaking of this size, there are a number of people who deserve special recognition. First among them is Nasheed Amin, who critiqued <u>Master Key to the GRE</u> in its entirety and whose insightful recommendations significantly enhanced all five volumes. We would also like to recognize the contributions of Seth Alcorn, Shawn Magnuson, Bronwyn Bruton, and Jessica Rider Amin. Without their assistance, this project would not have been possible. Finally, we would like to extend our gratitude to the students and instructors of Sherpa Prep, whose feedback, questions, and experiences lie at the heart of these materials.

Good luck with your preparation! If we can be of further assistance, please reach out to us at **jay@sherpaprep.com** or **nafeez@sherpaprep.com**. We'd love to hear from you.

On behalf of everyone at Sherpa Prep,

Jay

Jay Friedman
Founder
Sherpa Prep

Nafeez

Nafeez Amin
President
Sherpa Prep

Table of Contents

Volume 3

Word Problems

Chapter 1

Introduction to the GRE

Introduction

To be discussed:

Master Key to the GRE

Get a sense of how to use our books, how to study properly for the GRE, and how to access our online video content.

1 Choosing the Right Guide
2 Why Master Key is Special
3 How to Use Our Guides

4 Proper Study Habits
5 The App
6 Register Your Book!

The Structure & Scoring System

Read about the structure and scoring system of the GRE. Learn how to sign up for the exam and report your scores.

7 The Structure of the GRE
8 The Scoring System

9 Registering for the GRE
10 Reporting & Canceling Scores

Navigating the Exam

Get an in-depth sense of how the GRE's scoring system works and what you can do to maximize your performance on test day.

11 How the Exam Works
12 The Scoring Algorithm

13 Strategy & Time Management
14 Practice Tests

Intro to Quantitative Reasoning

Before you get started, educate yourself about the sort of math you'll find on the GRE and the four ways in which the exam formats its math questions.

15 Content Overview
16 Problem Solving Questions
17 "Select One or More" Questions

18 Numeric Entry Questions
19 Quantitative Comparisons
20 Before You Get Started

Master Key to the GRE

(1) Choosing the Right Guide – If you're like most people preparing to take the GRE, you probably have little sense of what differentiates one GRE guide from another.

• You may think that all GRE guides are more or less the same, or that the guides you see in bookstores are the most comprehensive on the market.

> ➤ The basic story is that most guides fall into one of two categories: "strategy-based" or "content-based".

• **The guides that you find in bookstores are almost always strategy-based.** In general, strategy-based guides provide:

> 1. A brief discussion of each question type that you find on the GRE.
> 2. A small set of suggestions for approaching these question types.
> 3. A collection of one hundred or so practice questions with some brief solutions.

• You also tend to find instructions on how to register for the GRE and report your scores; advice for the test day experience; and a few appendices that review vocabulary and elementary math principles.

> ➤ You won't find a lot of "know-how", however, in strategy-based guides. **The focus of such books is test-taking advice, not education.**

• The latest "premier" guide of one well-known test-prep provider, for example, devotes just nineteen pages to explaining math concepts.

• This said, you will find some useful ideas for taking the exam strategically, among them: ways to use the answer choices to your advantage; advice on how to pace yourself; and recommendations on how to read.

> ➤ In our experience, learning these sorts of strategies is helpful for most test-takers. Unfortunately, **they will not help you attain a strong GRE score, on their own**.

• If you do not know how to solve the problems you find on your exam, you will not do well, regardless of how well you can eliminate irrational answers, pace yourself, or otherwise "game" the exam.

> ➤ In contrast, **content-based guides teach the "know-how" you need** to solve exam questions without guessing.

• Such guides generally devote several pages of discussion to most of the major topics tested by the GRE.

• At the end of each discussion, you tend to find a set of section-ending exercises that allow you to practice what you've studied. As a result, content-based guides almost always have far more practice questions than their strategy-based counterparts.

> ➤ In our view, **this sort of approach is critical to success on the GRE**. It may not be the only thing you need to succeed, but it is the most important.

• Think about it logically for a moment. Is there any other exam you would dare take without learning its content beforehand?

• Of course not. Yet students regularly "prep" for the GRE using books that do not review the content of the exam. It takes years to graduate from college, and some admissions committees weigh GRE scores more heavily than grade point averages. Isn't an exam that means so much worth preparing for properly?

> ➤ Unfortunately, there a number of drawbacks to the content-based guides currently available for the GRE.

• For starters, **these guides almost always ignore the tactics recommended by strategy-based guides**, tactics that we believe are an asset to any test taker.

• What's more, such guides rarely tell you how frequently a particular topic is tested. Knowing which topics to study is important if you only have limited time to prepare for the GRE!

> ➤ Most importantly, none of the guides actually teach you EVERYTHING tested by the GRE.

• While most cover the major topics found on a typical exam, **none cover the vast array of rare and advanced concepts that you need to grasp if you're hoping to score <u>above</u> the 90th percentile.**

(2) Why Master Key Is Special – <u>Master Key to the GRE</u> is the only guide to the GRE that will teach you everything you need to attain a perfect score.

• Whether you're looking for help with advanced concepts, or are starting from scratch, our materials will have what you need.

> ➤ **We start by assuming you know NOTHING.** Everything is laid out for you as if you haven't done math in years.

• Each chapter focuses on a specific topic, such as Fractions, Rates, or Triangles, and opens with a thorough discussion of its simplest, most fundamental concepts.

• Bit by bit, we gradually explore ALL the wrinkles associated with that topic, so that you can solve problems involving sophisticated nuances, not just easy problems.

> ➤ At the ends of our chapters, you'll find a treatment of **every RARE and ADVANCED concept tested by the GRE.**

• You won't find these topics discussed anywhere else. <u>Master Key to the GRE</u> is the only resource that covers them.

• We know that some of you only need help solving the most difficult questions — the questions that determine who scores ABOVE the 90th percentile. We've made sure that our guides teach <u>everything</u>, so that students in your position get all the support they need.

> ➤ To keep things simple, we discuss math in **language that's EASY to understand** and focus on **SMART strategies for every level of material.**

• In writing <u>Master Key to the GRE</u>, we were determined to make our guides helpful for everyone, not just math geeks.

• We are GRE specialists who have spent our entire professional careers making math ACCESSIBLE to students who hate it. **These books are the culmination of over three decades of daily classroom instruction.** No matter how difficult a topic may be, we walk you through each concept, step by step, to ensure that everything makes sense.

> ➤ Along the way, **we sprinkle in hundreds of SHORTCUTS and TRICKS** that you won't find in any other guide.

• We know that TIME is a major concern for many test-takers, so we've included every time-saving strategy out there to help you "beat the clock".

- We don't care how well you think you know math. These shortcuts will save you valuable minutes, no matter what your current skill level may be.

    ➢ To complement our content-oriented approach, the first volume of <u>Master Key to the GRE</u> devotes **an entire chapter to something we call "Plan B" strategies**.

- A "Plan B" strategy is a strategy that can help you deduce a correct answer when you don't know how to solve a problem.

- Such "tricks of the trade" are sometimes encountered in mainstream strategy-based guides. No other guide, however, features a collection like the one we've put together here. We've got all of the tricks, not just a few.

    ➢ We also complement our content-oriented approach by telling you **how FREQUENTLY the GRE tests every concept** — something no other guide does.

- We know that most people don't have the time to study everything and aren't looking for a perfect score — just a score that's good enough to get them into the school of their choice.

- So, we let you know which topics are <u>commonly tested</u> and which ones are not so that you can determine for yourself which topics are worth your time.

    ➢ Additionally, **we organize our discussions by level of DIFFICULTY**, as well as by topic.

- As we see it, test-takers deserve to know which topics they need to master in order to get elite scores and which topics they can afford to skip if they're only looking for above average scores.

- Our hope is that by organizing our material in this way, you'll be able to limit your efforts to material that is right for you.

    ➢ In total, <u>Master Key to the GRE</u> includes **nearly ONE THOUSAND practice questions**. That's more than any other resource out there.

- Like our teaching sections, our practice questions are sorted by difficulty, as well as by topic, so that you can focus on any level of material and on any topic that you like.

- Moreover, nearly a quarter of these questions involve the most rare or advanced topics tested by the GRE. So if you're looking for a lot of help with diabolical fare, you'll find it here.

➢ Most of the solutions to these questions come in the form of **ANIMATED VIDEOS, which you can play on any computer, tablet, or smart phone**.

• We understand that the short, written explanations found in other GRE handbooks are often insufficient for students who find math challenging.

• By providing you with video solutions, we are able to talk you through our practice problems, every step of the way, so that you can follow along easily and see where your solution went wrong.

➢ In many cases, you'll find that our animated videos discuss **multiple ways to solve a question**.

• In math, there is often more than one way to solve a problem. Not all of these approaches, however, are equally efficient.

• Our videos discuss the best of these approaches to ensure that you're exposed to a solution that's not only fast and simple, but also works well with your way of thinking.

➢ We know that Master Key to the GRE is the most expensive GRE guide on the market.

• It's anywhere from $60 to $100 dollars more expensive than most of the alternatives out there. That's a lot of money.

• But let us ask you this. Which would rather have: an extra $60 to $100 dollars or the GRE scores that you need?

➢ Remember, it took you years to graduate from college, and many admissions committees weigh GRE scores more heavily than your grade point average.

• Isn't an exam that means so much worth the cost of a college textbook? Of course it is.

• If you're still not certain, **we encourage you to compare our materials to anything else** that you can find. Whether you're looking for help with advanced material or something a little less extreme, we have no doubt that you'll see why Master Key to the GRE is worth the difference.

(3) How to Use Our Guides – As mentioned, <u>Master Key to the GRE</u> has been designed to help you solve EVERY question on the GRE.

• It explains ALL of the TOUGH concepts that no other GRE prep book attempts to cover, not just the easy ones.

> ➤ Depending on your goals, however, you may NOT need to master everything. Not every program requires a perfect score. In fact, most don't require anything close.

• If you've yet to do so, we strongly encourage you to contact the programs you're interested in to see what sort of scores they require.

• Knowing "how high" to set the bar will give you a sense of whether you need to cover everything or just the core material. (Remember, we'll tell you how frequently each topic is tested!)

> ➤ Every volume of <u>Master Key to the GRE</u> has been designed to help someone starting from SCRATCH to build, step by step, to the most challenging material.

• Thus, Chapter 1 is intended to precede Chapter 2, and the same is true for each volume: <u>Arithmetic & "Plan B" Strategies</u> (Vol. 1) is intended to precede <u>Number Properties & Algebra</u> (Vol. 2).

• The chapters, however, are largely independent of one another, as are the books, so you're welcome to skip around if you only need help with a few key topics or are short on time.

> ➤ As you study, bear in mind that you DON'T have to master one topic before studying another.

• If you have a hard time with something, put it aside for a day or two. It can take one or two "exposures" for a concept to "click" – especially if it's new or tricky.

• You also don't need to solve all 1,000 of our practice problems. If you're comfortable with a topic, feel free to skip the questions marked "fundamental" to save time.

> ➤ Finally, remember that our ADVANCED materials are intended for students in need of PERFECT scores.

• If that's not you, don't waste your time! Questions involving advanced topics are generally rare for the GRE, so if you'd be thrilled with a score around the 90th percentile, you're more likely to achieve it by focusing on questions and materials involving core concepts.

(4) Proper Study Habits – Whatever your goals may be for the GRE, it's important that you work consistently.

• Studying a little EVERY DAY is the best way to retain what you're learning and to avoid the burn out that comes with studying too intensely for too long.

 ➢ In a perfect world, we'd have you study about an hour a day during the workweek and one to two hours a day on the weekends.

• Unfortunately, we know that such a schedule is unrealistic for some people. If you can't find an hour each day, at least DO SOMETHING!

• Even 5 minutes a day can help you stave off rust and prevent the cycle of guilt and procrastination that comes from not studying.

 ➢ If you can, do your best to AVOID CRAMMING. Much of what you'll be studying is boring and technical. It will take "elbow grease" to master.

• We truly question how much of this information can be absorbed in a few short weeks or in study sessions that last three or four hours.

• In our experience, most students who do too much too rapidly either burnout or fail to absorb the material properly.

 ➢ To avoid "study fatigue", SWITCH things up. Spend part of each day studying for the math portion of the exam and part for the verbal portion.

• And do your best to incorporate at least part of your study routine into your daily life.

• If you can study 30 minutes out of every lunch break and a few minutes out of every snack break, we think you'll find that you have more time to prepare than you might believe. We also think you'll find the shorter study sessions more beneficial.

 ➢ As you study, be sure to bear in mind that QUALITY is just as important as QUANTITY.

• Many test-takers believe that the key to success is to work through thousands of practice questions and to take dozens of exams. This simply isn't true.

- While working through practice questions and taking exams are important parts of preparing for the GRE, doing so does not mean that you are LEARNING the material.

  ➢ It is equally important that you LEARN from your MISTAKES. Whenever you miss a practice question, be sure to watch the video explanation that we've provided.

- Then, redo the problem yourself. Once you feel that you've "got it", come back to the problem two days later.

- If you still get it wrong, add the problem to your "LOG of ERRORS" and redo it every few weeks. Keeping track of tricky problems and redoing them MORE THAN ONCE is a great way to learn from your mistakes and to avoid similar difficulties on your actual exam.

  ➢ As you prepare, keep the REAL exam in mind. The GRE tests your ability to recognize concepts under TIMED conditions. Your study habits should reflect this.

- If it takes you 3 minutes to solve a problem, you may as well have missed that problem. 3 minutes is too much time to spend on a problem during an actual exam. Be sure to watch the video solutions for such problems and to redo them until you can solve them quickly.

- Likewise, bear in mind that you will take the GRE on a COMPUTER, unless you opt to take the paper-based version that is administered only three times a year.

  ➢ So adopt GOOD HABITS now. Whenever you practice, avoid doing things you can't do on a computer, such as writing atop problems or underlining key words.

- And make a NOTECARD whenever you learn something. The cards don't have to be complicated – even a sample problem that illustrates the concept will do.

- As your studying progresses, it can be easy to forget concepts that you learned at the beginning of your preparation. Notecards will help you retain what you've learned and make it easy for you to review that material whenever you have a few, spare minutes.

  ➢ Finally, do your best to keep your emotions in check. It's easy to become overconfident when a practice exam goes well or to get down when one goes poorly.

- The GRE is a tough exam and improvement, for most students, takes time.

- In our experience, however, test-takers who prepare like PROFESSIONALS — who keep an even keel, who put in the time to do their assignments properly, and who commit to identifying their weaknesses and improving them – ALWAYS achieve their goals in the end.

(5) The App – <u>Master Key to the GRE</u> is available in print through Amazon or through our website at **www.sherpaprep.com/masterkey**.

• It's also available as an app for iPhones and iPads through Apple's App Store under the title <u>GRE Math by Sherpa Prep.</u>

➤ Like the printed edition, the app comes with access to all of our LESSONS, practice QUESTIONS, and VIDEOS.

• And, like any book, it allows you to BOOKMARK pages, UNDERLINE text, and TAKE NOTES.

• Unlike a book, however, it also allows you to design practice quizzes, create study lists, make error logs, and keep statistics on just about everything.

➤ The ⬛ **DESIGN a PRACTICE QUIZ** ⬛ feature lets you make quizzes in which you select the TOPICS, the NUMBER of questions, and the DIFFICULTY.

• It also allows you to SHUFFLE the questions by topic and difficulty and to SET a TIMER for any length of time.

• For example, you can make a 30-minute quiz comprised of fifteen intermingled Ratio, Rate, and Overlapping Sets questions, in which all the questions are advanced. Or you can make a 10-minute quiz with just ten Probability questions, of which some are easy and others are intermediate. You can pretty much make any sort of quiz that you like.

➢ AFTER each quiz, you get to REVIEW your performance, question by question, and to view video solutions.

• You also get to see the difficultly level of your quiz questions, as well as the time it took you to answer each of them.

• You even get to COMPARE your performance to that of other users. You see how frequently other users were able to solve the questions on your quiz and how long it took them, on average, to do so.

➢ As you read through our lessons, the MAKE a STUDY LIST feature allows you to form a personalized study list.

• With the tap of a button, you can add any topic that you read about to an automated "to do" list, which organizes the topics you've selected by chapter and subject.

• From your study list, you can then access these topics instantly to revisit them whenever you need to.

➢ Similarly, the CREATE an ERROR LOG feature allows you to compile a list of practice problems you wish to redo for further practice.

• Every time you answer a question, you can add it to this log, regardless of whether you got the question right or wrong, or left it blank.

• By doing so, you can keep track of every problem that you find challenging and redo them until they no longer pose a challenge.

➢ Finally, the app TRACKS your PERFORMANCE at every turn to help you identify your strengths and weaknesses.

• In addition to the data from your practice quizzes, the app provides key information on how you're performing, by TOPIC and across DIFFICUTLY LEVELS.

• So if you want to know what percentage of advanced level Algebra questions you're answering correctly, the app can tell you. Likewise, if you want to know what percentage of intermediate level Triangle questions you're answering correctly, the app can tell you that too.

➢ The app offers the first volume of Master Key to the GRE for FREE. The other four volumes retail for $9.99 apiece.

(6) Register Your Book! – Every volume of <u>Master Key to the GRE</u> comes with six months of free access to our collection of video solutions.

- If you have a print edition of <u>Master Key</u>, you'll need to ⬚Register⬚ your book(s) to access these videos.

    ➢ To do so, please go to **www.sherpaprep.com/activate** and enter your email address, last name, and shipping address.

- **Be sure to provide the SAME last name and shipping address that you used to purchase your copy of <u>Master Key to the GRE</u>.**

- If you received your books upon enrolling in a GRE prep course with ⬚**Sherpa Prep**⬚, be sure to enter the same last name and shipping address that you used to enroll.

    ➢ Once you've entered this information, you will be asked to create an account password.

- Please RECORD this password! You will need it to login to our website whenever you choose to watch our videos.

- Our login page can be found at **www.sherpaprep.com/videos**. We recommend that you BOOKMARK this page for future visits.

    ➢ If your registration is ⬚**Unsuccessful**⬚, please send your last name and shipping address to **sales@sherpaprep.com**.

- We will confirm your purchase manually and create a login account for you.

- In most cases, this process will take no more than a few hours. Please note, however, that requests can take up to 24 hours to fulfill if you submit your request on a U.S. federal holiday or if we are experiencing extremely heavy demand.

    ➢ Six months after your date of registration, your video access to <u>Master Key to the GRE</u> will come to an end.

- An additional six months of access can be purchased at a rate of $9.99 per book. To do so, simply login at **www.sherpaprep.com/videos** and follow the directions.

About the GRE

(7) The Structure of the GRE – Before examining the content of the GRE, let's take a moment to discuss how the exam is structured and administered.

- The GRE is a computer-based exam that is offered world-wide on a daily basis.

  ➢ The test consists of six sections and takes around 3 hours and 45 minutes to complete (not including breaks).

- These sections are as follows:

  I.   An Analytical Writing section containing two essays.
  II. Two Verbal Reasoning sections.
  III. Two Quantitative Reasoning sections.
  IV. One Unidentified Research section.

- The Analytical Writing section is always first, while **the other five sections may appear in ANY order.** You get a 10-minute break between the third and fourth sections, and a 1-minute break between the other test sections.

  ➢ The Unidentified Research section **does NOT count towards your score** and is either a Verbal Reasoning section or a Quantitative Reasoning section.

- Unfortunately, the Unidentified Research section is designed to look exactly like the other sections — there is no way to spot it.

- As such, you must take all five sections seriously. Even though one of them will not count towards your score, there is no way of knowing which section that is.

  ➢ Finally, some exams have an **Identified Research section** in place of the Unidentified Research section.

- This section is marked "For Research Purposes" and does not count towards your score. If your exam has an Identified Research section, it will appear at the end of the test.

- On the following page, you'll find a breakdown of all six sections. Notice that every Quantitative Reasoning section has 20 questions and is 35 minutes long.

- Similarly, notice that every Verbal Reasoning section also has 20 questions but is only 30 minutes long.

  ➤ When viewing the table below, remember that **the order of sections 2 through 6 is RANDOM**. These sections can occur in any order.

- This means that the Unidentified Research section can be ANY section after the first and that you might get two Quantitative sections in a row (or two Verbal sections)!

Section	Task	Number of Questions	Time	Note
1	Analytical Writing	Two Essays	30 minutes per essay	
2	Verbal Reasoning	20	30 minutes	
3	Quantitative Reasoning	20	35 minutes	
10-minute break				
4	Verbal Reasoning	20	30 minutes	
5	Quantitative Reasoning	20	35 minutes	
6	Unidentified Research	20	30 or 35 minutes	Not scored

- Also remember that that Unidentified Research section may be replaced with an Identified Research section. If so, the Identified Research section will appear at the end of the test.

(8) The Scoring System – After your GRE has been completed and graded, you will receive three scores:

1. A Verbal Reasoning score.
2. A Quantitative Reasoning score.
3. An Analytical Writing score.

• **Both the Verbal Reasoning and Quantitative Reasoning scores are reported on a scale from 130 to 170, in one-point increments**.

  ➢ The Analytical Writing score is reported on a scale from 0 to 6, in half-point increments.

• A score of NS (no score) is given for any measure in which no questions (or essay prompts) are answered.

• In addition to these scaled scores, you will also receive percentile rankings, which compare your scores to those of other GRE test-takers.

  ➢ Before applying to graduate school or business school, you should have a basic sense of what constitutes a good score and what constitutes a bad score.

• Currently, **an average Verbal Reasoning score is 151, an average Quantitative Reasoning score is 152, and an average Analytical Writing score is approximately 3.5**.

• Roughly two-thirds of all test-takers receive a score within the following ranges:

1. Verbal Reasoning: 142 to 159
2. Quantitative Reasoning: 143 to 161
3. Analytical Writing: 3 to 4.5

  ➢ As a loose guideline, these ranges suggest that any score in the 160s is fairly exceptional and that any score in the 130s may raise a red flag with an admissions committee.

• The same goes for Analytical Writing scores higher than 4.5 or lower than 3. In fact, only 7 percent of test-takers receive a score above 4.5 and only 9 percent receive a score below 3.

• You can find a complete concordance of GRE scores and their percentile equivalents on page 23 of this document: **http://www.ets.org/s/gre/pdf/gre_guide.pdf**.

➤ As you prepare for the GRE, we strongly encourage you to research the programs to which you plan to apply.

• Get a general sense of what sorts of scores your programs are looking for. See whether they have "cutoff" scores below which they no longer consider applicants.

• Knowing what you need to achieve is important. If your program needs an elite math score, it's best to know immediately so that you can make time to prepare properly!

➤ In some cases, you'll find the information you need online. In many cases, however, you'll need to contact your program directly.

• If you are reluctant to do so, bear this in mind: many programs are more forthcoming about scores in person or over the phone than they are by email or on the internet.

• Moreover, it never hurts to make contact with a prospective program. Saying "hi" gives you a chance to ask important questions and — if you can present yourself intelligently and professionally — to make a good impression on a potential committee member.

➤ If a school tells you they are looking for applicants with an average score of 160 per section, remember that such quotes are only averages!

• Some applicants will be accepted with scores below those averages and some will be turned down with scores above them.

• An average is simply a "ballpark" figure that you want to shoot for. Coming up short doesn't guarantee rejection (particularly if the rest of your application is strong), and achieving it doesn't ensure admission.

➤ Unfortunately, not all programs are willing to divulge average or "cutoff" GRE scores to the public.

• If that's the case with a program you're interested, here are some general pointers to keep in mind:

1. Engineering, Economics, and Hard Sciences programs are likely to place far more emphasis on your Quantitative Reasoning score than your other scores.

2. The more prestigious a university it is, the more likely its programs will demand higher scores than comparable programs at other schools.

3. Public Health, Public Policy, and International Affairs programs likely require very strong scores for all three portions of the GRE.

4. Education, Sociology, and Nursing programs are less likely to require outstanding scores.

➢ Should you wish to get a sense of average GRE scores, by intended field of study, you can do so here: **http://www.ets.org/s/gre/pdf/gre_guide_table4.pdf**.

• When viewing these scores, remember that these are the scores of INTENDED applicants!

• The average score of ACCEPTED applicants is likely to be higher for many programs — in some cases, much higher.

➢ Finally, it's worth noting that many programs use GRE scores to determine which applicants will receive SCHOLARSHIPS.

• When contacting programs, be sure to ask them about the averages or "cutoffs" for scholarship recipients.

• And if you find it difficult to study for an exam that has little to do with your intended field of study, just remember: strong GRE scores = $$$!

(9) Registering for the GRE – The GRE is administered via computer in over 160 countries on a near daily basis.

• This means that you can that you take the GRE almost ANY day of the year.

> ➤ To register, you must create a personalized GRE account, which you can do online at **http://www.ets.org/gre/revised_general/register/**.

• When creating your account, the NAME you use must MATCH the name you use to register for the GRE.

• **It must also match the name on your official identification EXACTLY**! If it doesn't, you may be prohibited from taking the exam (without refund).

> ➤ We encourage you to schedule a date that gives you ample time to prepare properly. Don't choose a random date just to get it over with!

• If possible, wait until you score a few points higher than your target score at least TWO TIMES in a row on practice exams. Doing so will ensure that you're ready to take the exam.

• When scheduling the time of day, **don't schedule an 8 a.m. exam if you are not accustomed to waking up at 6:30 a.m. or earlier**. The exam is challenging enough. Don't take it when you're likely to be groggy or weary!

> ➤ If you plan to take the exam on a specific date, register at least one month in advance. Exam centers have limited capacity, so dates can fill up quickly, especially in the fall.

• On the day of the test, be sure to bring your official identification and your GRE admission ticket.

• Once you register for the exam, your admission ticket can be printed out at any time through your personalized GRE account online.

> ➤ Finally, if you need to reschedule or cancel your exam date, you must do so no later than FOUR days before your test date. (Ten days for individuals in mainland China.)

• This means that a Saturday test date must be canceled by Tuesday and that an April 18th test date must be canceled by April 14th.

• You can find more information on canceling or rescheduling a test date here: **http://www.ets.org/gre/revised_general/register/change**.

(10) Reporting & Canceling Scores – Immediately upon completing your exam, you will be given the opportunity to cancel your scores or to report them.

- If you choose to cancel your scores, they will be deleted irreversibly.

  ➢ Neither you nor the programs to which you're applying will see the numbers. Your official score report, however, will indicate a canceled test.

- In general, there's almost no reason to cancel your scores.

- **The GRE has a Score Select option that allows you to decide which scores to send if you've taken the GRE more than once**. Thus, if you take the exam a second time (or a third time), you can simply choose which set of scores to report.

  ➢ If you choose to report your scores, you will immediately see your unofficial Quantitative Reasoning and Verbal Reasoning scores.

- Roughly 10 to 15 days after your test date, you will receive an email notifying you that your official scores and your Analytical Writing score are available.

- To view them, simply go to the personalized GRE account you created to register for the exam.

  ➢ You won't need to memorize any school CODES to send your scores while at the test center.

- Such codes will be accessible by computer, should you wish to report your scores when you're there. To get the code for a particular program, you'll need:

  1. The name of the college (e.g. College of Arts & Sciences).
  2. The name of the university.
  3. The city and state of its location.

- As long as you have this information for each of your programs, you'll have everything you need to send out your score reports on the spot.

  ➢ **Your OFFICIAL and UNOFFICIAL scores are unlikely to differ**. If they do, the difference will almost surely be a single point.

- For example, your Verbal Reasoning score may rise from a 157 to a 158 or your Quantitative Reasoning score may dip from a 162 to a 161.

- The scores you receive on test day are an estimate comparing your performance with previous data. The official scores compare your performance with those of everyone who took that particular exam – hence the potential discrepancy.

> **Your official scores will be valid for FIVE years**. For example, a test taken on August 2nd, 2015 will be valid until August 1st, 2020.

- Over the course of those five years, your scaled scores will never change. The percentiles, however, may shift marginally.

- Thus, a scaled Verbal Reasoning score of 162 may equate to the 89th percentile in 2015. Come 2018, however, that 162 may equate to a 91st percentile.

> On test day, after viewing your unofficial scores, you will be given a choice at the test center.

- You can choose NOT to send your scores at that time or to send **free score reports** to as many as FOUR graduate programs or fellowship sponsors.

- If you choose to send out score reports at the test center, you will be given two further options:

1. The **Most Recent** option – send your scores from the test you've just completed.
2. The **All** option – send the scores from all the GREs you've taken in the last five years.

> After your test date, you can send additional score reports for a fee. **For each report**, you will be given the options above.

- **You will also be given the option to send your scores from just one exam OR from ANY exams you've taken over the last five years.**

- You cannot, however, choose your best Quantitative Reasoning score from one exam and your best Verbal Reasoning score from another. When sending scores, you must send all the scores you receive on a particular exam date.

> ➢ Given all of these options, **here's our advice**. First, NEVER cancel your scores. There's no point.

• Even if you believe you've had a bad performance, you may as well learn how you did. You never know — you might even be pleasantly surprised.

• If your scores are great, you're done. Send out your scores on test day to take advantage of the four free score reports.

> ➢ If you feel you can do better, retake the exam as soon as possible. Don't let your hard work go to waste.

• Anyone can have a bad day, misplay their time, or make an uncharacteristic number of careless errors.

• **You can retake the exam every 21 days** and up to 5 times within any 12-month period, so you won't have to wait long.

> ➢ Upon receiving your second set of scores, use the Score Select option on test day to determine which set of scores to send for free (or to send both sets).

• In the unpleasant event that you take the exam more than twice, consider utilizing the Score Select option the day after your last exam.

• This will allow you to send the single set of scores (or pair of scores) that puts you in the best possible light. Of course, if that last score is awesome, use the four free score reports to send out your most recent scores while you're at the test center!

Navigating the Exam

(11) How the Exam Works – Although the GRE is administered on computer, the exam has been designed to mimic the experience of a traditional, paper-based standardized test.

- This means that you can:

  - ☑ Skip questions and return to them later.
  - ☑ Leave questions blank.
  - ☑ Change or edit an answer.

- You can even "flag" questions with a check mark as a reminder to revisit them before time expires. (As with a paper-based exam, however, you cannot return to a section once that section ends.)

  - ➤ If you took the GRE before 2011, you'll notice that this format differs dramatically from the one you remember.

- **The exam is no longer adaptive on a question-by-question basis**, so the problems don't get harder if you answer a prior problem correctly.

- In fact, you can now preview every question within a section the moment that section begins. (If you like, you can even do the problems in reverse order.)

  - ➤ There are, however, a few differences between the way the GRE works and that of most paper-based standardized tests.

- First, the questions in each section do NOT get progressively harder.

- Unlike, say, the SAT, where the first questions within a section are generally easy and the last questions within a section are generally hard, **the difficulty of GRE questions varies throughout a particular section**. In other words, a section might start with a hard question and end with an easy question.

  - ➤ Furthermore, the GRE has a "Review Screen" that allows you to see which questions you've answered and which ones you haven't.

- The Review Screen can also be used to see which questions you've flagged for further review. (A very helpful feature!)

> ➤ **Finally, the GRE adapts on a section-by-section basis.** If you perform well on your first quantitative section, your second quantitative section will be harder.

• Likewise, if you do not perform well on your first quantitative section, your second quantitative section will be easier.

• The verbal sections work this way, too. The quantitative and verbal sections, however, are independent of one another. A strong performance on a verbal section will not result in more difficult quantitative sections, or vice versa.

> ➤ According to our experiments with the GRE's official test software, **how you perform on your first quantitative section can produce 1 of 3 results.**

• The same is true of your performance on the first verbal section:

Approximate # of Correct Questions on First Section	Difficulty Level of Second Section
0 to 6	Easy
7 to 13	Medium
14 to 20	Hard

• In some exams, it might take 15 correct answers to end up with a hard second section. In others, it might take 13. The correlation between the number of questions you get right and the difficulty level of your second section, however, generally matches the chart above.

> ➤ Our experiments also indicate that **the difficulty of the questions that you get right has no bearing on the difficulty level of the second section**.

• In other words, getting any 14 (or so) questions correct will give you a hard second section — it doesn't matter whether those questions are the hardest 14 or the easiest 14.

• It also doesn't matter how quickly you answer anything. There are no bonus points for solving problems quickly.

> ➤ It should, however, be noted that **a hard second section is not comprised entirely of hard questions,** nor an easy second section entirely of easy questions.

• The questions in ANY section span a range of difficulties. A hard second section simply has a greater number of hard questions than an easy one. Thus, if you receive easy questions in your second quantitative section, it does not mean that you've done poorly!

(12) The Scoring Algorithm – Exactly how the GRE is scored is a closely guarded secret.

• From the official practice test software, however, it's clear that Quantitative Reasoning and Verbal Reasoning scores are essentially the byproducts of two factors:

    1. How many questions you answer correctly.
    2. Whether your second sections are easy, medium, or hard.

• As you may recall from our discussion of the structure of the GRE, every exam has two Quantitative Reasoning sections and two Verbal Reasoning sections that count.

    ➢ Since each of these sections has 20 questions, every GRE has 40 Quantitative Reasoning questions and 40 Verbal Reasoning questions.

• As you may also recall, each of these measures is scored on a 41-point scale (from 130 to 170). This means, that **each question is essentially worth 1 point**.

• Thus, to get a Quantitative Reasoning score of 170, you likely need to answer all 40 questions correctly. Each question that you get wrong more or less subtracts 1 point from your score.

    ➢ In analyzing the practice test software, however, it's also apparent that there are deductions for failing to achieve a hard or medium second section.

• In general, these deductions range from 1 to 3 points.

• For example, if you were to get 11 questions correct on your first Quantitative Reasoning section, your score would be lowered 9 points on account of the 9 questions you got wrong or left blank since the exam treats blank and incorrect answers equally. (**There is NO PENALTY for getting problems wrong, so always GUESS when you're stuck!**)

    ➢ Your 11 correct answers, however, would also result in a second section of medium difficulty.

• Thus, your score would be lowered an additional 1 to 3 points for failing to make it to the hard section.

• Likewise, if you were to answer only 4 questions correctly in your first Quantitative Reasoning section, your score would be lowered 16 points for the blank or incorrect answers, 1 to 3 points for failing to make it to the hard section, and another 1 to 3 points for failing to make it to the medium section.

➢ Thus, a test taker who gets 10 questions right in each of his or her Quantitative Reasoning sections would likely receive a score from 147 to 149.

• The 20 questions left blank or answered incorrectly would deduct 20 points from the total score.

• Failing to make it to the hard section would deduct an additional 1 to 3 points. Subtracted from 170 (a perfect score), this would leave a final score of 147 to 149:

170	A perfect score
10	10 missed questions in section 1
10	10 missed questions in section 2
− 1 to 3	The penalty for not reaching the hard section
147 to 149	

➢ In all likelihood, the scoring algorithm considers a few other factors as well.

• For example, when exam-makers opt to include a greater number of difficult questions on a particular exam, they likely slide the scale for that exam 1 to 2 points in order to normalize its data with past exams that contain fewer difficult questions.

• From what we've seen, however, the dynamics described above will predict your score perfectly in most instances.

(13) Strategy & Time Management – Given the factors we've just discussed, there are several tactics that we recommend when taking the GRE.

1. SKIP around.

• It doesn't matter which questions you get right, so you may as well work on the questions that are easiest for you first.

> ➤ **Don't waste your time on a question that you don't understand or that confuses you.**

• Engaging such questions will only take time from questions that may be easier for you. If you come across something that makes you nauseous, FLAG IT and double back after you've solved the questions that you know how to solve.

2. FOCUS on your FAVORITE 15.

• As we've seen, there are potentially harsh deductions for failing to achieve a hard or medium second section.

> ➤ Since reaching the hard second section generally demands a minimum of 13 to 15 correct responses, we encourage you to focus your efforts on the 15 easiest questions.

• You shouldn't ignore the hardest 5 questions, but you should save them for last. **If you don't think you can answer 15 questions correctly, focus your efforts on the easiest 10 questions**. Landing in the lowest tier can devastate your score.

3. GUESS on questions that you don't understand.

• We've also seen that an incorrect answer is no worse than a blank answer, so you may as well <u>guess</u> on anything that you don't understand and flag it for further review. Remember, there's no penalty for guessing!

> ➤ As you'll see, **there's either a 1 in 5 chance or a 1 in 4 chance of guessing most GRE questions correctly.**

• Those chances increase if you can eliminate a couple of answer choices through logic. If you have time left over, you can return to the questions you've flagged after you've answered everything else.

4. REMEMBER the "Two-and-a-Half Minute Rule".

• Over the years at Sherpa Prep, we've noticed that test-takers who take more than 2.5 minutes to solve a question do so correctly only 25% of the time.

> ➤ Given that there are usually five answers to choose from, the odds of guessing correctly are 20%. If you can eliminate bad answer choices, those odds rise further!

• We know that it's tempting to battle questions to the end, especially if you "think" you can solve them. **Stubbornly hanging on, however, is a sure way to MANGLE your score.**

• Doing so wastes time (time that could be used to solve other problems) and is no more likely to result in a correct answer than guessing.

> ➤ So, if you find yourself stuck on a particular question, do yourself a favor: flag the question, then guess.

• If you can eliminate answer choices before doing so, great. Obeying the "2.5 minute rule" will help you save time for the questions at the end of the exam and avoid the debilitating panic that comes upon realizing that you've squandered your time.

5. Don't work TOO QUICKLY.

• We know that time is a critical factor on the GRE and that the exam-makers don't give you much of it.

> ➤ **Working at a frenzied pace, however, will only result in one thing — careless errors. A lot of them.**

• The key to saving time is obeying the "2.5 minute rule" and learning the right way to solve each type of problem – not working at breakneck speeds.

• If you know how to solve a problem, take the time to do so properly. You may not have time to triple check your work, but you do have time to work through any problem with care.

> ➤ **Watch out, however, for any question that you can solve in 10 seconds or fewer.**

• While there are plenty of GRE problems that can be solved in 10 seconds, exam-makers often design questions to take advantage of quick assumptions. Taking an extra 10 seconds to ensure that you haven't missed something is a great way to catch potential traps!

(14) Practice Tests – As you work through <u>Master Key to the GRE</u>, we strongly encourage you to take a practice exam every week or two.

• Success on the GRE is not just the byproduct of mastering its content — it also demands good test-taking skills.

> ➤ **Taking practice exams will help you build stamina and improve your time management**.

• Remember, the GRE takes nearly four hours to complete. Learning how to deal with the fatigue you'll encounter is part of the battle!

• The same is true of the pacing of the exam. If you don't master the speed at which you need to work, you can easily sabotage your score by working too quickly or too leisurely.

> ➤ Before you take the GRE, we encourage you to **take a minimum of SIX practice exams**.

• If you're like most test-takers, you'll need anywhere from six to eight practice exams to properly familiarize yourself with the GRE.

• For the first few — don't bother with the essays. As you begin your preparation, your time is better spent studying new material and reviewing what you've learned. Towards the end of your preparation, however, your practice exams should be full-blown dress rehearsals.

> ➤ **There are a number of different practice exams available online. Of these, only two are produced by the ETS, the company that designs the GRE.**

• At no cost, you can download the software that runs these exams from the following address: **http://www.ets.org/gre/revised_general/prepare/powerprep2/**.

• These exams have been designed to work on both Macs and PCs. As long as your computer's operating system and software are reasonably up to date, you should be able to use them on any computer.

> ➤ For additional exams, almost any of the available options will do. While they all have issues of one sort or another, most are reasonable facsimiles of the GRE.

• When taking such exams, however, please bear in mind that they are NOT the real thing. Some of their questions are unrealistic and their score predictions, though roughly accurate, are best taken with a grain of salt.

➤ Whenever you take a practice exam, it's important that you **make the experience as REALISTIC as possible**.

• Doing things you can't do on test day will only corrupt your practice results and prevent you from adopting helpful habits.

• If you can, take each exam in one sitting and resist the urge to pause the test or to use outside help. Likewise, refrain from drinking or eating during your tests. No coffee, no water, no snacks. Save these things for your 10-minute break between sections 3 and 4.

➤ Remember, you're preparing for a stressful "brain marathon" that's essentially 4-hours long. You'll need STAMINA to be successful.

• Figure out how much you need to eat and drink before your test. Figure out what to eat during your break. Identify the kind of foods that suit you best.

• The same goes for your bathroom habits. At the exam center, you can't pause the test to go to the bathroom. So, use your practice exams to learn how your eating habits affect your bodily needs! "Holding it in" for over an hour is a brutal way to take this test.

➤ As you take your practice exams, do your best to **stay off the "emotional rollercoaster"**. Don't get too high when things go well.

• And don't get too down if your scores don't shoot up instantly. Improving GRE scores is hard work.

• For some people, progress is a slow, steady crawl. For others, it's an uneven process, filled with periods of stagnation, occasional drops, and dramatic increases.

➤ However your exams may be going, keep grinding away! Stay focused on your goals and keep up the hard work.

• Test-takers who prepare like professionals — who keep an even keel, who do their assignments properly, and who commit to improving their weaknesses — ALWAYS achieve their goals in the end.

• As we tell our students, preparing for the GRE is like going to the gym. It may take you a while to get in shape, but ANYONE can do so if they put in the time and train properly.

➤ **After you complete each practice exam, go through it carefully and learn from your mistakes**.

• See whether you can identify any trends in your performance. Are you working too quickly and making careless errors? Are you struggling with the same topics repeatedly?

• Are you running out of time because you're violating the "2.5 minute rule"? Do you start off strong and then taper off as the test goes along? Does it take you half an hour to get "locked in" and then get better as you go?

➤ A lot of people believe they are "bad test-takers". This is nonsense. The reality is that people get questions wrong for tangible reasons.

• Analyzing your mistakes when the "game is real" will allow you to PINPOINT those reasons so you can ADDRESS them.

• To help you become a more "self-aware" test-taker, we encourage you to fill out the following table every time you complete an exam:

	Knew How to Solve	Didn't Know How to Solve
Correct	Bravo!	Luck
Incorrect	Carelessness?	**Expected**

➤ If you get a question wrong because you don't know how to solve it, see whether you can identify its TOPIC or notice any TRENDS.

• For example, you might notice that a lot of your mistakes involve Algebra. If so, that's a clear indication that you need to improve your Algebra skills.

• If you get a question wrong despite knowing how to solve it, see whether you can figure out how it happened. Did you misread the question? Did you write down information incorrectly? Did you make a silly math error?

➤ Mistakes such as these are often the result of RUSHING, which in turn is generally the byproduct of poor time management elsewhere.

• So keep track, to the best of your abilities, of whether you are finishing your sections too quickly or are making frantic efforts to finish because you're violating the "2.5 minute rule" too frequently. Both scenarios generally lead to a host of careless mistakes that will sabotage your progress.

Intro to Quantitative Reasoning

(15) Content Overview – The quantitative portion of the GRE is designed to measure your ability to think <u>smartly</u> about math — to find simple solutions to problems that seem complicated.

• The problems that you'll encounter may appear difficult or time-consuming, but there's ALWAYS a straightforward way to solve them.

➢ In terms of content, the GRE solely tests concepts that you learned in high school or use in everyday life.

• These concepts fall into four categories:

1. Arithmetic, Algebra, and Number Properties
2. Word Problems
3. Data Interpretation
4. Geometry

➢ You won't find any Calculus or Trigonometry on the GRE, nor will you find some of the more sophisticated forms of Algebra typically taught in an Algebra II course.

• That's because the emphasis of this exam is on your ability to reason.

• By limiting the content to the topics listed above, the GRE becomes less about "what you know" (everyone studied those topics in high school) and more about your ability to APPLY commonly known information and to think logically.

➢ This said, don't be fooled into thinking that GRE math can't be sophisticated. The exam demands that you know these topics EXTREMELY well.

• To be successful on the GRE, you'll need to relearn everything you learned about them (or were supposed to learn) back in high school.

• And, if you want to solve the most advanced questions, you'll need to learn a few intricacies that you almost surely were never taught.

➤ Based on our analysis of the official exam materials released to the public, roughly one-third of GRE questions focus on Arithmetic, Algebra, and Number Properties.

• Approximately 33% are Word Problems and a little more than a third involve Geometry or the interpretation of Charts and Graphs:

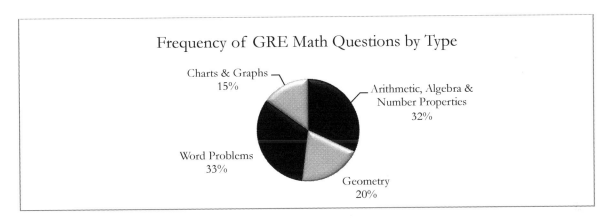

• When viewing the diagram above, bear in mind that Word Problems and problems involving Geometry or Charts and Graphs often demand the use of Algebra and Arithmetic. Thus, in many ways, Algebra and Arithmetic are even more critical to your success than the diagram above suggests.

➤ Volume 1 of <u>Master Key to the GRE</u> is devoted to **Arithmetic & "Plan B" Strategies**.

• Here, you'll find discussion of such topics as:

Arithmetic Shortcuts	Strategies for "Smart Math"
Essential Number Lists	Strategies for Using the Answer Choices
Fractions	Number Picking Strategies
Decimals	Strategies for Guessing
Digit Problems	

➤ Volume 2 is dedicated to **Number Properties & Algebra**. Among the topics you'll find covered are:

Factors & Multiples	Exponents & Roots
Prime Factorization	The Properties of Evens & Odds
Number Line Problems	Algebra
Absolute Value	Functions, Sequences & Symbolism
Remainder Problems	

➢ Our discussion of **Word Problems** is divided between Volumes 3 and 4. Volume 3 focuses on topics such as:

Percents	Algebraic Word Problems
Mixtures	Age Problems
Alterations	Overlapping Sets
Ratios & Proportions	Exponential & Linear Growth
Rate Problems	

• Volume 4 examines **Statistics & Data Interpretation**.

➢ Among the various chapters of Volume 4, you'll find discussions of a wide range of topics, including:

Means, Medians & Modes	Probability
Weighed Averages	Combinatorics
Standard Deviation	Bar Graphs & Line Graphs
Quartiles & Boxplots	Pie Charts & Data Tables
Normal Distributions	Multi-Figure Data Sets
Equally Spaced Number Sets	

• Finally, Volume 5 is devoted to **Geometry**.

➢ Here, you'll find a detailed treatment of everything you may have been taught in high-school but have probably forgotten.

• The major topics include:

Lines & Angles	Rectangular Solids
Triangles	Cylinders
Quadrilaterals	Coordinate Geometry
Polygons	
Circles	

• If all of this seems intimidating, don't worry! We promise you: <u>Master Key to the GRE</u> will show you just how simple these concepts can be.

(16) Problem Solving Questions – Before we get started, let's take a few pages to discuss the ways in which the GRE formats its math questions.

• As you may recall, every GRE has two Quantitative Reasoning sections. Since each of these sections has 20 questions, your exam will feature a total of 40 math questions (that actually count).

  ➢ 25 of these will be "Problem Solving" questions and 15 will be "Quantitative Comparison" questions.

• If you've taken standardized tests before, Problem Solving questions will be familiar to you. Here's an example:

If $x + y > 14$ and $x = 2y + 8$, then which of the following must be true?

(A) $y < -3$ **(B)** $y < -2$ **(C)** $y = 0$ **(D)** $y > 2$ **(E)** $y > 4$

Answer: D. To answer questions in this format, you simply need to select the answer choice that represents the correct answer.

  ➢ Here, for example, we've been told that $x = 2y + 8$. Thus, we can rewrite $x + y > 14$ as follows, by substituting $2y + 8$ for x:

Replace x with $2y + 8$

$\longrightarrow (2y + 8) + y > 14$

• To simplify the Algebra, we can drop the parentheses and subtract 8 from both sides of the inequality. Doing so proves that the correct is (D), since:

$2y + 8 + y > 14$	Drop the parentheses.
$2y + y > 6$	Subtract 8 from both sides.
$3y > 6$	Add $2y + y$.
$y > 2$	Divide both sides by 3.

• If the math doesn't make sense here, don't worry! This question is simply intended to show you what a Problem Solving question looks like. The math behind it is covered in our book on Number Properties & Algebra.

(17) "Select One or More" Questions – From time to time, Problem Solving questions will prompt you to select one or more answer choices.

- On a typical exam, each quantitative section will contain (at most) one or two of these questions.

  ➢ "Select One or More" questions are easy to spot — they always ask you to "indicate <u>all</u> such values".

- What's more, **the answer choices are always in square boxes**. In regular Problem Solving questions, the answer choices are circled.

- According to the Official Guide to the GRE revised General Test, the directions for such questions are always as follows:

  <u>**Directions:**</u> **Select ONE or MORE answer choices according to the specific directions.**

- If the question does not specify how many answer choices to select, you must select ALL that apply. The correct answer may be just one of the choices or as many as all of the choices. **There must, however, be at least one correct answer.**

  ➢ The exam-makers further specify that no credit is given unless you select all of the correct answers and no others. In other words, there is NO PARTIAL credit.

- Thus, if there are two correct answers, and you only select one, the GRE gives you zero credit. The same is true if there are three correct answers and you select four.

- Let's take a look at a sample question:

  If $-2 \leq x \leq 8$ and $-4 \leq y \leq 3$, which of the following could represent the value of xy?

  Indicate <u>all</u> such values.

  | A | -40 | B | -32 | C | 7 | D | 15 | E | 32 |

Answer: B, C, and D. Notice that there are two clues indicating that we may need to select more than one answer here.

- First, the question asks us to "indicate <u>all</u> such values". **Additionally, the answer choices are in boxes.**

  ➢ To answer this question, we first need to determine the range of possible values for xy.

- We can do so by identifying the greatest and smallest possible values for x and y.

- According to the problem, $-2 \leq x \leq 8$ and $-4 \leq y \leq 3$. Thus, the greatest and smallest values for each variable are:

$$x = -2 \text{ and } 8 \qquad\qquad y = -4 \text{ and } 3$$

  ➢ Next, we can **test all four combinations** of x times y to determine the largest and smallest values of xy.

- If x can be as small as -2 and as large as 8, and y can be as small as -3 and as large as 4, then those combinations would be:

Combo #1	Combo #2	Combo #3	Combo #4
$(-2)(-4) = 8$	$(-2)(3) = -6$	$(8)(-4) = -32$	$(8)(3) = 24$

  ➢ As we can see from these combinations, the greatest possible value of x times y is 24 and the smallest possible value is -32.

- Thus, the range of values for xy extends from -32 to 24. Algebraically, this can be stated as $-32 \leq xy \leq 24$.

- Since -32, 7, and 15 all fall within the range of value from -32 to 24, **we must select** $\boxed{B}$, $\boxed{C}$, **and** $\boxed{D}$, **and nothing more, to get credit for this question**. If we fail to select all three answer choices, or select a fourth, our response would be considered incorrect.

  ➢ Again, if the math doesn't make sense here, don't worry! This question is simply intended to show you what a "Select One or More" question looks like.

- The math behind it is covered in our book on Number Properties & Algebra.

(18) Numeric Entry Questions – On each of your quantitative sections, anywhere from one to three of your Problem Solving questions will ask you for a "Numeric Entry".

- Numeric Entry questions prompt you to **type a numeric answer into a box** below the problem.

  ➤ Such questions tend to be more difficult than other Problem Solving questions since you can't use the answer choices to determine whether you're on the right track.

- Further, it's almost impossible to guess the correct answer. With regular Problem Solving questions, you at least have a 1 in 5 chance of getting lucky.

- Let's take a look at a sample question:

  When walking, a person takes 24 complete steps in 15 seconds. At this rate, how many steps does this person take in 5 seconds?

- There are several ways to solve a problem like this. Perhaps the easiest way is to set up a proportion:

$$\frac{24 \text{ steps}}{15 \text{ seconds}} = \frac{x \text{ steps}}{5 \text{ seconds}}$$

- When comparing the bottoms of the two fractions, notice that "15 seconds" is exactly three times as large as "5 seconds".

  ➤ With proportions, the relationship between the tops of the fractions is the same as that between the bottoms.

- In other words, "24 steps" must be three times as large as "x steps", since "15 seconds" is three times as large as "5 seconds".

- Thus, $x = 8$, because 24 is three times as large as 8. To solve this problem, therefore, **we would need to type 8 into the numeric entry box** beneath the question.

  ➤ As with the previous sections, don't worry if the math doesn't make sense here! This question is simply intended to show you what a Numeric Entry question looks like.

- The math behind it is covered properly in our book on Word Problems.

(19) Quantitative Comparisons – The rest of your math questions will prompt you to compare two quantities.

• Such questions, commonly known as "Quantitative Comparisons", consist of two quantities, labeled Quantity A and Quantity B, and, in many cases, some additional information.

   ➢ Beneath the two quantities you'll find four answer choices, asking which of the two quantities is LARGER. The answer choices are always the SAME.

• **MEMORIZE them IMMEDIATELY**. 15 of your 40 math questions will be in this format. If you spend 10 seconds wading through the answer choices on each of these questions, you'll be wasting 2.5 minutes of your exam!

• Let's take a look at a sample problem:

$$xy \geq 1$$

Quantity A   **Quantity B**

   xy $(xy)^3$

   (A) **Quantity A is greater.**
   (B) **Quantity B is greater.**
   (C) **The quantities are equal.**
   (D) **The relationship cannot be determined from the information given.**

Answer: D. At the top of the problem, we are told that $xy \geq 1$. This means that xy can be any value equal to or greater than one.

   ➢ If $xy = 1$, notice that the quantities are equal, since $(1)^3 = 1 \times 1 \times 1 = 1$. If $xy = 2$, however, notice that Quantity B is greater than Quantity A, since $(2)^3 = 2 \times 2 \times 2 = 8$.

• Because the two quantities can be equal or can be different, we cannot determine which quantity is larger from the given information. The correct answer is therefore (D).

• Any time two quantities have an INCONSISTENT RELATIONSHIP — i.e. any time that A can be greater than or equal to B or that B can be greater than or equal to A — the relationship between the two quantities CANNOT be determined.

(20) Before You Get Started – If you've read through the preceding pages, you're ready to get started.

- Before you do, we'd like to offer you a last few bits of advice. We know that many people who take the GRE are not very comfortable with math.

  ➢ If you're one of them, you may have been told at an early age that you weren't a "math person" or that your brain "doesn't work that way".

- That's total nonsense. The truth is that EVERYONE can learn the sort of math required by the GRE.

- Yes, it may require hard work — especially if you haven't done math in over a decade. But you CAN do it. Don't let the idiotic assessment of a bad teacher or a misogynist prevent you from attaining your goals.

  ➢ As you begin to practice, **DON'T try to do everything in your head**. Scratch work is an IMPORTANT part of the problem solving process.

- Taking notes will SPEED you up and help you avoid careless errors.

- Make sure, however, that your writing is organized and legible. Sloppy handwriting is a sure path to careless errors. Writing the work for one problem atop the work for another problem is even worse. (Yes, some people do this.)

  ➢ Likewise, **make sure that your handwriting is appropriately sized**. If you can solve twenty problems on a single sheet of paper, your writing is too small.

- Yes, the GRE only provides you with a few sheets of unlined scratch paper, but you can always raise your hand to trade for new sheets BEFORE you run out.

- Conversely, if you're using one sheet of paper per question, write smaller. You shouldn't need to request paper frequently. Divide your sheets of scratch paper into six equal sections. With proper penmanship, you should be able to fit the work for any problem in one of the sections.

  ➢ When solving problems, **beware of crazy decimals or fractions**. If your scratch work involves something like $0.123 \times \frac{7}{13}$, you're doing something wrong.

- In general, the GRE tends to use "smart numbers" — numbers that are designed to yield simple results under the proper analysis.

- When the GRE uses exotic numbers, the exam is almost always testing your ability to identify patterns or relationships (e.g. $0.\overline{54} = \frac{5}{9}$) or to approximate.

  ➤ If you're worried about anxiety, preparing THOROUGHLY for the GRE is the best way to beat test-taking jitters.

- Nothing calms unsteady nerves more than seeing problems you KNOW how to solve because the content is EASY for you.

- You should also **set up a test date that allows you enough time to schedule a retake**, if necessary. (Remember, you can take the GRE every 21 days and up to 5 times a year.) Knowing that you'll have a second shot at the GRE can take the pressure off your first exam.

  ➤ On test day, bring food and water with you to the exam center. You'll be there for nearly five hours.

- Doing anything for that length of time is fatiguing. Eating a few nuts and a piece of fruit before your exam (and during your break) will help keep you sharp.

- Just be sure to steer clear of drinking too much water or consuming too much sugar or caffeine. You don't want to take multiple bathroom breaks while your exam is running or to crash during the final hour of your test.

  ➤ If you can, **get to the test center early**. Taking the GRE is stressful enough. You don't want to exacerbate that stress by running late.

- Plan to get there a half hour in advance. If you're commuting to an unfamiliar area, research the commute carefully and allot an additional 15 minutes (in case you get lost).

- Once inside (don't forget your ID and admissions ticket!), use the extra time to warm up with a few practice problems or to review your notes. Doing so will help get your brain "in gear" before your exam.

  ➤ Finally, **brace yourself for broken air-conditioners, sniffling neighbors, and unfriendly staffers**.

- Although test centers are generally well run, it's important to remember that there can be problems.

- As long as you dress in layers, however, and make use of the headphones or earplugs that are supplied with your exam, these issues shouldn't pose you any problems.

Chapter 2

Percents

Percents

To be discussed:

Fundamental Concepts

Whether you're aiming for a perfect score or a score closer to average, mastery of the following concepts is essential.

1 Introduction
2 Taking a Percent of a Number
3 Calculating a Percent Change
4 Original Value vs. New Value
5 Consecutive Percents
6 PUQ's: Percents with Unspecified Quantities
7 "Part-to-Whole" Percents
8 Percent "Greater or Less Than"
9 Summary

Rare or Advanced Concepts

The following concepts are either advanced or are tested only on rare occasions. If you don't need an elite math score, don't waste your time!

10 Interest Problems
11 Alterations
12 Mixtures
13 The Weighted Average Shortcut

Practice Questions

There's no substitute for elbow grease. Practice your new skills to ensure that you internalize what you've studied.

14 Drills
15 Problem Sets
16 Solutions

Fundamental Concepts

(1) Introduction – The word *percent* is composed of the prefix *per*, which means "divide", and the root *cent*, which means "a hundred".

$$\frac{x}{100}$$

- In other words, the term *percent* is simply a way of saying "divided by 100" or "out of 100". Thus, when we say that "25% of John's marbles are red", we're saying that if John were to have 100 marbles, exactly 25 would be red.

$$\frac{25}{100}$$

  ➢ To work with percents, you must be able to CONVERT them to fractions and decimals.

- To convert a **percent to a fraction**, simply DIVIDE it by 100. To convert a **percent to a decimal**, SHIFT its decimal point TWO places to the left:

$$17\% = \frac{17}{100} = 0.17 \qquad 123\% = \frac{123}{100} = 1.23 \qquad 300\% = \frac{300}{100} = 3.00$$

  ➢ Should a percent contain a DECIMAL, nothing changes! Divide the percent by 100 to make it a fraction or shift its decimal two spaces to the left to make it a decimal:

$$0.33\% = \frac{0.33}{100} = \frac{33}{10,000} = 0.0033 \qquad 12.5\% = \frac{12.5}{100} = \frac{125}{1,000} = 0.125$$

- Likewise, if a percent contains a FRACTION, either divide it by a 100 and simplify the result OR convert it to a decimal and shift the decimal point two spaces to the left:

Divide by a Hundred	OR	Convert to a Decimal

$$\frac{1}{4}\% = \frac{\frac{1}{4}}{100} = \frac{1}{4} \times \frac{1}{100} = \frac{1}{400} \qquad\qquad \frac{1}{4}\% = 0.25\% = 0.0025$$

  ➢ Note that to convert **fractions and decimals INTO percents**, we have to REVERSE these steps.

- Thus, to convert a decimal into a percent, SHIFT the decimal point TWO spaces to the right:

$$0.27 = 27\% \qquad\qquad 0.003 = 0.3\% \qquad\qquad 10.00 = 1,000\%$$

- Likewise, to convert a fraction into a percent, MULTIPLY it by 100:

$$\frac{2}{5} \rightarrow \frac{2}{5} \times 100 = \frac{2}{5} \times (20) = 40\% \qquad \frac{9}{4} \rightarrow \frac{9}{4} \times 100 = \frac{9}{4} \times (25) = 225\%$$

$$\frac{0.4 \times \frac{Y}{100}}{100}$$

> ➤ When solving percent problems, ALWAYS CONVERT PERCENTS into fractions or decimals.

- Exam-makers intentionally design problems to trip up test-takers who neglect to do so. Here's a typical example:

0.4 percent is equal to which of the following?

(A) $\frac{1}{400}$ (B) $\frac{1}{250}$ (C) $\frac{3}{200}$ (D) $\frac{1}{4}$ (E) $\frac{2}{5}$

Answer: B. Although 0.4% may appear to equal $\frac{4}{10}$, it does not. Remember, to convert a percent into a fraction, you have to <u>DIVIDE it by 100</u>. Doing so here proves that (B) is the correct answer, since:

$$0.4\% = \frac{0.4}{100} = \frac{4}{1,000} = \frac{1}{250}$$

> ➤ If you need to convert a TRICKY FRACTION into a percent, simply use the "Conversion List".

- As you may recall from our book on <u>Arithmetic & "Plan B" Strategies</u>, the "Conversion List" is a small table of fractions and their decimal equivalents:

$\frac{1}{2} = 0.5$	$\frac{1}{5} = 0.2$	$\frac{1}{8} = 0.125$	$\frac{1}{11} = 0.\overline{09}$
$\frac{1}{3} = 0.\overline{3}$	$\frac{1}{6} = 0.1\overline{6}$	$\frac{1}{9} = 0.\overline{1}$	$\frac{1}{99} = 0.\overline{01}$
$\frac{1}{4} = 0.25$	$\frac{1}{7} \approx 0.14$	$\frac{1}{10} = 0.1$	$\frac{1}{100} = 0.01$

- Knowing this list will allow you to convert difficult fractions into percents quickly and easily. For example, if you know that $\frac{1}{8} = 0.125$, then you can deduce that $\frac{3}{8} = 37.5\%$, since:

$$\frac{3}{8} = 3 \times \frac{1}{8} = 3 \times 0.125 \rightarrow 0.375 \times 100 = 37.5\%$$

- Likewise, if you know that $\frac{1}{7} \approx 0.14$, then you can deduce that $\frac{6}{7} \approx 86\%$, since:

$$\frac{6}{7} = \frac{7}{7} - \frac{1}{7} \approx 1 - 0.14 \rightarrow 0.86 \times 100 = 86\%$$

> ➤ On a final note, it's worth pointing out that 100% = 1. It may feel wrong, but it has to be true since:

$$100\% = \frac{100}{100} = 1$$

(2) Taking a Percent of a Number – The fastest way to take the percent of a number is with the "10% Shortcut".

- As you may recall from our book on <u>Arithmetic & "Plan B" Strategies</u>, if you can get 10% of a number, you can get other percents of that number (e.g. 5%, 15%, 20%, etc.) very easily.

  ➢ To get 10% of a number, simply SLIDE the decimal spot ONE space to the left:

  $$10\% \text{ of } 82 = 8.2 \qquad 10\% \text{ of } 230 = 23 \qquad 10\% \text{ of } 0.05 = 0.005$$

- To get 5% of a number, therefore, simply take HALF of 10%:

  $$5\% \text{ of } 270 = \frac{1}{2} \text{ of } 27 = 13.5 \qquad\qquad 5\% \text{ of } 38 = \frac{1}{2} \text{ of } 3.8 = 1.9$$

- Similarly, to get 15% of a number, ADD 10% and 5% together:

  $$15\% \text{ of } 220 \rightarrow 10\% + 5\% = 22 + \left(\frac{1}{2} \text{ of } 22\right) = 22 + 11 = 33$$

- Likewise, to get 20%, 30%, or 40% of a number, get 10% of that number and double, triple, or quadruple it.

  $$20\% \text{ of } 180 \rightarrow 10\% \times 2 = 18 \times 2 = 36 \qquad 60\% \text{ of } 110 \rightarrow 10\% \times 6 = 11 \times 6 = 66$$

  ➢ If you can get 1% of a number, the "10% shortcut" can also be used to determine more complicated percents, such as 6%, 11%, or 29%.

- To get 1% of a number, simply SLIDE its decimal spot TWO spaces to the left:

  $$1\% \text{ of } 82 = 0.82 \qquad 1\% \text{ of } 230 = 2.30 \qquad 1\% \text{ of } 0.05 = 0.0005$$

- Thus, to get 11% of a number, add 10% and 1% together:

  $$11\% \text{ of } 120 \rightarrow 10\% + 1\% = 12 + 1.2 = 13.2$$

- Likewise, to get 29% of a number, subtract 1% from 30%:

  $$29\% \text{ of } 40 \rightarrow (10\% \times 3) - 1\% = (4 \times 3) - 0.4 = 11.6$$

- In general, you SHOULDN'T need to determine 1% of a number very often (if at all). Still, it can come in handy every now and then. As always, just be sure you're not missing an easier approach before using it!

- Another great way to "take a percent of a number" is to convert a percent to a FRACTION.

- In math, the word OF means "MULTIPLY". Therefore, statements such as "40% of 30" and "70% of 200" can be thought of as:

$$\frac{40}{100} \times 30 \qquad\qquad \frac{70}{100} \times 200$$

- Once a percent is in fraction form, any ZEROES in common to the tops and bottoms of the fraction and number can be CANCELED. Thus:

$$\frac{40}{100} \times 30 = \frac{4\cancel{0}}{1\cancel{00}} \times \frac{3\cancel{0}}{1} = 4 \times 3 = 12 \qquad \frac{70}{100} \times 200 = \frac{70}{1\cancel{00}} \times \frac{2\cancel{00}}{1} = 70 \times 2 = 140$$

- The "**Fraction Approach**" to percents is particularly effective with more complicated percents.

- Imagine that you needed to determine "14% of 350" or "22% of 30":

$$\frac{14}{100} \times 350 \qquad\qquad \frac{22}{100} \times 30$$

- After canceling the zeroes, you would only need to BREAK DOWN the remaining numbers to determine the percentages. Thus:

$$\frac{14}{10\cancel{0}} \times 35\cancel{0} = \frac{\cancel{2}(7)}{\cancel{2}(\cancel{5})} \times \cancel{5}(7) = 49 \qquad \frac{22}{10\cancel{0}} \times 3\cancel{0} = \frac{22}{10} \times 3 = 2.2 \times 3 = 6.6$$

  ➢ We highly recommend that you learn BOTH strategies.

- Although the "10% Shortcut" is often the faster strategy (and the strategy that you should use more frequently), the "Fraction Approach" is a great complement to the "10% Shortcut".

- Some problems yield more easily to one approach than the other. Knowing both strategies is a huge help, especially when the numbers get funky.

(3) Calculating a Percent Change – GRE problems often involve percent changes.

- To calculate a percent change, first place the difference between the new and original values over the original value. Then MULTIPLY the result by 100 to CONVERT the fraction into a percent:

$$\text{Percent Change} = \frac{\text{Difference}}{\text{Original}} \times 100$$

> ➤ If the new value is GREATER than the original value, the percent change formula will measure the INCREASE in value.

- If the new value is LESS than the original value, the percent change formula will measure the DECREASE in value. Consider the following:

If a couch is purchased for $500 and resold for $300, what is the percent decrease in the value of the couch?

(A) 20% (B) 30% (C) 40% (D) 60% (E) 67%

Answer: C. The difference between the new and original values of the couch is $200, since $500 – $300 = $200. The original value of the course is $500. Thus, the value of the couch decreased 40%, as:

$$\frac{\text{Difference}}{\text{Original}} \times 100 = \frac{200}{500} \times 100 = \frac{2}{5} \times 100 = \frac{2}{5} \times 5(20) = 2 \times 20 = 40\%$$

> ➤ Be sure to note that the ORIGINAL value is always the value that is CHRONOLOGICALLY earlier.

- In the problem above, $500 is considered the original value, since the couch is initially purchased at a price of $500 before it is resold for $300. Beware: in more difficult problems, it is easy to confuse the new and original values. Consider the following:

Store *S* reported sales of $71,000 for May of this year. If the total sales for the same month last year was $40,000, what was the approximate percent change in sales?

(A) 8% (B) 23% (C) 45% (D) 75% (E) 87%

Answer: D. The difference in total sales is $31,000, since $71,000 – $40,000 = $31,000. Although the problem mentions $71,000 before it mentions $40,000, the original sales total is $40,000, since sales were $71,000 this year and $40,000 last year. Thus, the **approximate** percent change was 75%, since:

$$\frac{\text{Difference}}{\text{Original}} \times 100 = \frac{31,000}{40,000} \times 100 = \frac{31}{40} \times 100 \approx \frac{30}{40} \times 100 = \frac{3}{4} \times 100 = 75\%$$

WATCH OUT for percent change problems involving changes GREATER than 100 percent.

Such problems are very easy to misconstrue. When solving them, don't make assumptions. Treat them as you would any other problem involving a percent change.

- Consider the following:

In 1998, the value of a certain baseball card was $100. By 2005, the value of that card had risen to $300. From 1998 to 2005, by what percent did the value of the card increase?

(A) 3% (B) 50% (C) 100% (D) 200% (E) 300%

Answer: D. Although the value of the card tripled, the value only increased by 200%. The difference between the values is $200, since $300 − $100 = $200. Since the original value of the card is $100, the correct answer must therefore be (D), as:

$$\frac{\text{Difference}}{\text{Original}} \times 100 = \frac{200}{100} \times 100 = 2 \times 100 = 200\%$$

If this seems odd to you, just remember: if your salary doubles after you receive your graduate degree, it has <u>increased</u> by 100%, not 200%!

- Here's a more difficult example for you:

The cost of a certain house in 2005 was 200 percent of its cost in 2008.

Quantity A	**Quantity B**
The percent by which the cost of the house decreased	**50%**

Answer: C. To solve this question, first label the 2008 cost c. If the 2005 cost was "200% of the 2008 cost", **the 2005 cost must equal $2c$**, since:

$$\text{"200\% of } c\text{"} = \frac{200}{100} \times c = 2c$$

Furthermore, since **2005 occurred before 2008**, the cost of the house in 2005 must be the original value. Thus, the correct answer is (C), since the cost of the house <u>decreased 50%</u>:

$$\frac{\text{Difference}}{\text{Original}} \times 100 = \frac{2c - c}{2c} \times 100 = \frac{c}{2c} \times 100 = \frac{1}{2} \times 100 = 50\%$$

(If you don't remember how the answer choices work for a Quantitative Comparison question, be sure to visit section **19** of the Introduction!)

(4) Original Value vs. New Value – GRE percent problems will also ask you to apply a percent change.

• For example, a problem may tell you that a $120 stock increased its value by 30%, or that a "40% off" sale lowered the value of a sweater to $60.

> ➢ When the value of an object increases or decreases, the relationship between its ORIGINAL value and its NEW value can be stated as:

$$\text{Original} \times (1 \pm \% \text{ Change}) = \text{New}$$

• To understand why this is so, imagine that the value of x increased by 30%. The **new value** of x would equal its **original value + its increase**, or "100% of x" + "30% of x". Algebraically, this relationship can be stated as:

$$x + 0.3x \xrightarrow{\text{factor out } x} x(1 + 0.3) = 1.3x$$

Original value   Change   New value

• Now imagine that the value of x decreased by 40%. The **new value** of x would equal its **original value – its decrease**, or "100% of x" minus "40% of x". Algebraically, this relationship can be stated as:

$$x - 0.4x \xrightarrow{\text{factor out } x} x(1 - 0.4) = 0.6x$$

Original value   Change   New value

> ➢ If the percent change is an INCREASE, the value of that increase should be ADDED to 1. Conversely, if it's a decrease it should be SUBTRACTED from 1.

• For example, if the price of a $90 tennis racket increases by 20%, the **new price** of the tennis racket will equal the **original price × 1.2**, or $108, as:

$$\$90(1.2) = \$108$$

• Conversely, if the price of a $60 sweater decreases by 30%, the **new price** of the sweater will equal the **original price × 0.7**, or $42, as:

$$\$60(0.7) = \$42$$

Remember:
30% off = 70% of

➤ To simplify the arithmetic of such calculations, think of your original value as "**10 × something**". You can use this 10 to slide away the decimal point.

• For example, if the price of a $50 pair of shoes increases by 20%, the **new price** of the shoes will equal the **original price × 1.2**, or $60, as:

$$\$50(1.2) = 5\underbrace{(10)(1.2)}_{\text{multiply}} = 5(12) = \$60$$

• Likewise, if a $130 dress is marked down 70%, the **new price** of the dress will equal **original price × 0.3**, or $39, since:

$$\$130(0.3) = 13\underbrace{(10)(0.3)}_{\text{multiply}} = 13(3) = \$39$$

➤ When comparing the new value of an object to its original value, it is CRITICAL that you DETERMINE whether you know the original value or the new value.

• **It is very easy to mistake one for the other**. Asking yourself whether you've been given the original or new value will help you avoid common mistakes. Consider the following:

The population of town X rose by 20 percent from 1992 to 1994. If the total population of town X was 300 in 1994, what was its population in 1992?

(A) 240   (B) 250   (C) 320   (D) 350   (E) 360

Answer: B. Since 1992 predates 1994, the **original size** of the town is unknown. However, since the percent change in the town's population is 20% and the **new size** of the town is 300, we know that:

$$\text{original} \times (1.20) = 300$$

Thus, the size of the town in 1992 must have been 250, since dividing both sides by 1.2 gives us:

$$\text{original} = \frac{300}{1.2} = \frac{3,000}{12} = \frac{\cancel{X}(1,000)}{\cancel{X}(4)} = 250$$

➤ Finally, it's worth pointing out that with some problems you may find it easier to BYPASS the formula, "**original × (1 ± change) = new**".

• In fact, this may frequently be the case if YOU KNOW the ORIGINAL value, but not the final. Consider the following:

After taxes, the price of a certain meal was $60.

Quantity A	**Quantity B**
The price of the meal after a 15 percent tip	$70

Answer. B. There are two ways to solve this problem: we can use the formula "**original ×** **(1 ± change) = new**" or determine 15% of 60. Using the formula gives us:

$$60(1.15) = 6(10)(1.15) = 6(11.5) = 6(11) + 6(0.5) = 66 + 3 = \$69$$

Given the complexity of this calculation, however, it's probably easier to solve it using the "10% Shortcut". Doing so gives us:

$$15\% \text{ of } 60 \rightarrow 10\% + 5\% = 6 + 3 = 9$$

Since a $60 meal + a $9 tip = $69, the correct answer is (B).

> ➤ But BE CAREFUL. If you prefer the "10% Shortcut", be sure that you NEVER use it when you know the NEW value, but not the original.

• These sorts of problems MUST be solved with the formula. Using the "10% Shortcut" for such problems is a classic mistake. Consider the following:

The price of a pair of jeans is $85 when store *S* offers a 15% discount.

Quantity A	**Quantity B**
The price of the jeans without the discount	$92

Answer. A. The original price of the jeans is unknown and the change in its value is a 15% decrease. Since the new cost of the jeans is $85, we know that:

$$\text{original} \times (1 - 0.15) = \text{original} \times (0.85) = \$85$$

Thus, the price of the jeans without the discount must be $100, since:

$$\text{original} = \frac{\$85}{0.85} = \frac{8{,}500}{85} = \$100$$

Note that if we use the "10% shortcut" to remove 15% from $85 (a very common error), we mistakenly get that Quantity B is bigger than Quantity A, since the 85 − 15% of 85 = 72.75:

$$15\% \text{ of } 85 \rightarrow 10\% + 5\% = 8.5 + 4.25 = 12.75$$

(5) Consecutive Percents – Percent problems often involve a series of percent changes.

> ➤ Such problems can only be solved ONE STEP at a TIME.

• **Do not combine the changes!** You must calculate each percent change <u>individually</u>. Consider the following:

On Monday, the value of stock *K* rose 25 percent, but on Tuesday the value fell 20 percent. If the stock was valued at $40 per share at the start of the two-day period, what was the value of 10 shares of stock *K* at the end of the two-day period?

(A) $360   (B) $380   (C) $390   (D) $400   (E) $420

Answer: D. At the start of the two-day period, the price of a single share of stock *K* was $40. On Monday, its value **increased by** 25%. Thus, the value of the stock rose to $50, as:

$$\$40(1 + 0.25) = 40(1.25) = 4(10)(1.25) = 4(12.5) = \$50$$

On Tuesday, the value of the stock **decreased by** 20%. Thus, its value fell to $40, as:

$$\$50(1 - 0.2) = 50(0.8) = 5(10)(0.8) = 5(8) = \$40$$

Since the value of stock *K* at the end of the two-day period was $40, the value of 10 shares of that stock would be $400, as $40 × 10 = $400. Hence, the correct answer is (D).

> ➤ Note that if we were to combine the two percent changes into a single step, we would get a net increase of 5%, as 25% – 20% = 5%.

• However, a 5% increase in the value of a $40 stock would result in an **incorrect calculation** of $42 per share, since $40(1.05) = $42.

• Here's a second example for you:

If Bo spends 60 percent of a 50-dollar stipend on groceries and 10 percent of the remainder on stamps, what percent of the stipend does he have left?

(A) 12%   (B) 18%   (C) 24%   (D) 30%   (E) 36%

Answer: E. If Bo spends 60% of the $50 stipend, he **spends $30** and has **$20 left over**, as:

$$60\% \text{ of } \$50 = 0.6(50) = 0.6(10)(5) = 6(5) = \$30$$

Likewise, if Bo spends 10% of the **remainder** on stamps, he has $18 left, since 10% of $20 = $2, and $20 – $2 = $18. Thus, he has 36% of the stipend left, since $18 out of $50 = 36%:

$$\frac{18}{50} \times 100 = 18 \times 2 = 36\%$$

➤ Watch out for COMPARISON questions involving consecutive percent changes, particularly those with DIFFICULT numbers.

• For such questions, it's often better to set up the computations rather than crunch the numbers. Consider the following:

Quantity A	**Quantity B**
The value of a $175 stock that falls 20% and then rises 20% during week X	The value of a $175 stock that rises 20% and then falls 20% during week X

• To solve this question, we could raise 175 by 20%, lower it by 20%, and then reverse the steps to determine the value of Quantity B. Doing so, however, would involve a lot of work.

➤ Remember, the more busy work that a problem seems to require, the more likely it is that the problem has a smart, simple solution.

• To solve this problem quickly, let's first set up the computation for **Quantity A**, but avoid the arithmetic.

• If the value of a $175 stock falls 20%, the value equals 175(0.8). However, if this value then rises 20%, the final value must be:

$$175(0.8)(1.2)$$

➤ Next, let's set up the computation for **Quantity B**. If the value of a $175 stock rises 20%, the value equals 175(1.2).

• However, if this value then falls 20%, the final value must be:

$$175(1.2)(0.8)$$

• Since 175(0.8)(1.2) = 175(1.2)(0.8), the two quantities are equal. The correct answer, therefore, is (C).

(6) PUQ's: Percent with Unspecified Quantities – Previously, in our book on <u>Arithmetic</u> <u>& "Plan B" Strategies</u>, we introduced a type of problem that we like to call "PUQ's".

• As you may recall, the term "PUQ" is an acronym that is short for "**Percent** problems with **Unspecified Quantities**."

• In that discussion we suggested that the key to solving PUQ's is to pick numbers.

> ➤ Specifically, we recommended that you **pick 100** to make the arithmetic easy to work with.

• To recall the strategy properly, let's work through a practice problem:

The population of country X increased by 20 percent from 1984 to 1991 and decreased by 10 percent from 1991 to 1998. By what percent did the population of country X change from 1984 to 1998?

(A) 8 (B) 9 (C) 10 (D) 11 (E) 12

Answer. A. Since the exact population of country X is **unspecified**, let's pretend that the population of country X in 1984 equals 100.

A 20% **increase** in the size of the population would raise it from 100 to 120, since 20% of 100 = 20. Likewise, a subsequent decrease of 10% would then lower the population from 120 to 108, since 10% of 120 = 12.

To determine a percent change, we must place **the difference between the new and original values over the original value**, and then multiply the result by 100. Thus, the percent change in the population of country X from 1984 to 1998 was 8%, as:

$$\frac{\text{Difference}}{\text{Original}} = \frac{108 - 100}{100} \times 100 = \frac{8}{100} \times 100 = 8\%$$

> ➤ The reason we choose numbers to solve PUQ's is that doing so makes the math easy.

• We can solve problems like the one above by using variables to represent the unknown values. <u>Picking numbers, however, eliminates the need to set up equations and, therefore, is dramatically FASTER.</u>

➤ On occasion, you may encounter a question that looks like a "PUQ" but involves real numbers.

• Unfortunately, questions with concrete values are NOT PUQ's. **If your question involves REAL numbers, you CAN'T pick numbers**. In such cases, picking numbers may contradict information within the problem.

• Consider the following:

The price of a certain couch was recently reduced by 30 percent. If that couch is now $45 less expensive, what was the original price, in dollars, of the couch?

(A) 55   (B) 90   (C) 135   (D) 150   (E) 160

• Although this problem may seem like a PUQ, it is not: it contains the real value $45. Thus, **we cannot choose numbers**. If we were to let the value of the couch equal $100, it would contradict information within the question.

➤ After all, if a $100 couch is $45 less expensive, its price has NOT been reduced 30%, as the problem states.

• By picking $100 as the original value, the price of the couch is actually reduced 55%, violating the construct of the question.

• To solve this problem correctly, we must recognize that "30% of the original price" = $45. This "apples-to-oranges" relationship can be used to determine 100% of the original price by means of the following "percents-to-dollars" proportion:

$$\frac{30 \text{ percent}}{45 \text{ dollars}} = \frac{100 \text{ percent}}{x \text{ dollars}}$$

➤ The correct answer is therefore (D), since cross-multiplication proves that the price of the couch must have been $150:

$$30x = 45(100) \quad \rightarrow \quad x = \frac{45(100)}{30} = \frac{45(10)}{3} = \frac{\cancel{3}(15)(10)}{\cancel{3}} = \$150$$

• Alternatively, we can also solve this problem if we recognize that "30% × (unknown value) = $45". If we let the unknown value = x, we get:

$$0.3x = \$45 \quad \rightarrow \quad x = \frac{45}{0.3} = \frac{450}{3} = \$150$$

(7) "Part-to-Whole" Percents – "Part-to-whole" percent problems involve the relationship between (surprise!) a part and its whole.

- Imagine that you needed to determine "what percent of 250 is 45" or "35 percent of what number is 42".

  ➢ A simple way to solve such questions is to compare the part to the whole through the following PROPORTION:

$$\frac{\text{Part}}{\text{Whole}} = \frac{\text{Percent}}{100}$$

- For example, to determine "what percent of 250 is 45", we need to determine the **percent**. We've been given the **part** and the **whole**, so we can set up the relationship as:

$$\overset{\text{part}}{\underset{\text{whole}}{\frac{45}{250}}} = \overset{\text{percent}}{\frac{x}{100}}$$

- Thus, 45 is 18 percent of 250, since cross-multiplication gives us:

$$45(100) = 250x \;\rightarrow\; \frac{45(100)}{250} = x \;\rightarrow\; \frac{45(10)}{5(5)} = 9(2) = 18 = x$$

  ➢ Likewise, to determine "35 percent of what number is 42", we need to determine the **whole**.

- We've been given the **percent** and the **part**, so we can set up the relationship as:

$$\overset{\text{part}}{\underset{\text{whole}}{\frac{42}{x}}} = \overset{\text{percent}}{\frac{35}{100}}$$

- Thus, 35 percent of 120 is 42, as:

$$42(100) = 35x \;\rightarrow\; \frac{42(100)}{7(5)} = x \;\rightarrow\; 6(20) = 120 = x$$

- Every now and then you may come across a "part-to-whole" relationship in which the PART is LARGER THAN the WHOLE. For example, imagine that you needed to determine "what percent 64 is of 40". Since 64 is larger than 40, you might be tempted to assume that 64 is the whole.

➤ If you're confused about which value is the "part" and which is the "whole", simply remember that "IS = PART" and "OF = WHOLE".

• In other words, any "part-to-whole" relationship can also be thought of as:

$$\frac{\text{Is}}{\text{Of}} = \frac{\text{Percent}}{100}$$

• For example, to determine "what percent is 64 of 40", we need to determine the **percent**. We've been told "64 **is**" some percent "**of** 40", so the relationship between 64 and 40 is:

$$\frac{64}{40} = \frac{x}{100}$$

is → ← percent

of

• Thus, 64 is ⎡160 percent⎤ of 40, since cross-multiplying gives us:

$$64(100) = 40x \;\;\rightarrow\;\; \frac{64(100)}{8(5)} = x \;\;\rightarrow\;\; 8(20) = 160 = x$$

➤ Remembering that "IS = PART" and "OF = WHOLE" is particularly important as problems grow more difficult. Consider the following:

The price of a certain dress is 30 percent less than the price of a matching purse, and the price of a pair of shoes is 60 percent more than the price of the dress. What percent of the price of the purse is the price of the shoes?

(A) 89%   (B) 94%   (C) 97%   (D) 108%   (E) 112%

Answer: E. The prices of the dress, purse, and shoes are unspecified, so we can let the price of the **purse = 100**. If the price of the dress is 30% less than the price of the purse, the price of the **dress = 70**, as 100(0.7) = 70. Likewise, if the price of the shoes is 60% more than the price of the dress, the price of the **shoes = 112**, as 70(1.6) = 7(16) = 7(10 + 6) = 112.

The problem asks what percent "**OF** the purse **IS** the shoes". Thus, the relationship between the purse and the shoes is:

$$\frac{112}{100} = \frac{x}{100}$$

The price of the purse, therefore, is 112% the price of the shoes, since cross-multiplying gives us:

$$100(112) = 100x \;\;\rightarrow\;\; \frac{100(112)}{100} = 112 = x$$

(8) Percent "Greater or Less Than" – On occasion, percent questions may ask you to determine the percent by which one quantity is "greater or less than" another.

- Such questions are very similar to "calculating a percent change" questions, in which the difference between the new and original values is placed over the original value.

  ➤ To solve "percent greater or less than" questions, first place the DIFFERENCE between the two quantities over the "GREATER or LESS THAN" amount.

- Then multiply the result by 100 to convert the fraction into a percent:

$$\frac{\text{Difference}}{\text{"Greater or Less Than" Amount}} \times 100$$

- Imagine that you needed to determine "by what percent is 14 greater than 8". To do so, you would only need to place the difference between 14 and 8 over the "greater than" number, which is 8.

  ➤ We know that 8 is the "greater than" number since we've been told that 14 is "(some) percent **greater than 8**".

- In other words, 14 is 75% greater than 8, since:

$$\frac{\text{Difference}}{\text{Greater Than}} \times 100 \rightarrow \frac{6}{8} \times 100 \rightarrow \frac{3}{4} \times 100 = 75\%$$

- To get a better feel for percent "greater or less than" questions, consider the following:

In 2005, the sale of movie tickets grossed 2.8 billion dollars in revenue. In 2004, the sale of movie tickets grossed 3.2 billion dollars in revenue. The gross revenue from movie tickets in 2005 was what percent less than the gross revenue in 2004?

(A) 12.5%   (B) 12.9%   (C) 13.4%   (D) 13.8%   (E) 14.3%

Answer: A. The difference between 3.2 billion and 2.8 billion is 0.4 billion. Since the gross revenue in 2005 was "(some) percent **less than** the gross revenue in **2004**", the "less than" amount was the gross revenue in 2004, or 3.2 billion.

Thus, the 2005 gross revenue was 12.5% less than the 2004 gross revenue, as:

$$\frac{\text{Difference}}{\text{Less Than}} \times 100 \rightarrow \frac{0.4}{3.2} = \frac{1}{8} = 0.125 \times 100 = 12.5\%$$

(9) Summary – Percent problems contain a variety of wrinkles that are easily confused.

• Knowing "when to do what" can be difficult. To help keep the ideas straight, remember that all percent problems ask you to perform 1 of 4 tasks. These tasks are listed below in order of their frequency.

1. Take a percent of a number.

• Such questions are by far the most frequent. "Take a percent" questions provide you with **a specific percentage** and **an actual number**. You simply need to crunch the numbers. In most cases, the easiest way to do so is to use the "10% Shortcut". Thus, 15% of 70 = 10.5, since:

$$15\% \text{ of } 70 = 10\% + 5\% = 7 + \left(\frac{1}{2} \text{ of } 7\right) = 7 + 3.5 = 10.5$$

2. Calculate a percent change.

• "Calculate a percent change" questions ask you to determine the percent by which the final value has increased or decreased from the original. In other words, such questions do not provide you with a percent change: **the percent change is unknown**. To calculate the unknown percent change, be sure to use the percent change formula:

$$\frac{\text{Difference}}{\text{Original}} \times 100$$

• Thus, if the membership of a certain club rises from 20 to 30, the percent change in the club's membership would be 50%, since the difference between the two amounts is 10 and the original amount is 20:

$$\frac{10}{20} \times 100 = 0.5 \times 100 = 50\%$$

• Remember, **"percent greater or less than"** questions are a subset of "calculate a percent change" questions. To solve such questions, think of the "greater or less than" amount as the original quantity:

$$\frac{\text{Difference}}{\text{"Greater or Less Than" Amount}} \times 100$$

• Thus, to determine by what percent "24 is **greater than 18**", simply place the difference between 24 and 18 over the "greater than" amount:

$$\frac{6}{18} \times 100 = \frac{1}{3} \times 100 = 0.\overline{3} \times 100 = 33.\overline{3}\%$$

3. Apply a percent change.

• "Apply a percent change" questions differ from "calculate a percent change" questions in that "apply" questions **give you a percent change and ask you to use it**, whereas "calculate" questions ask you to figure out what the percent change was. The "apply a percent change" formula is:

$$\text{Original} \times (1 \pm \text{Change}) = \text{New}$$

• When using the formula, convert the percent change into a decimal and add or subtract the change from 1. **Be sure to determine whether you've been given the original amount OR the new amount.** Thus, a $40 pair of shoes that decreased in value by 20% has a new value of $32, since:

$$40(1 - 0.2) = 40(0.8) = 4(8) = 32.$$

4. Work with a percent relationship.

• "Work with a percent relationship" questions involve "part-to-whole relationships". A simple way to solve such questions is to compare the part to the whole through the following proportion:

$$\frac{\text{Part}}{\text{Whole}} = \frac{\text{Percent}}{100}$$

• If you're confused about which value is the "part" and which is the "whole", simply remember that "IS = PART" and "OF = WHOLE". For example, if the projected attendance at a show is 120, but the actual attendance is only 90, to determine "what percent **OF** the projected attendance **IS** the actual attendance", simply express the relationship as:

$$\overset{\text{is}}{\underset{\text{of}}{\frac{90}{120}}} = \overset{\text{percent}}{\frac{x}{100}}$$

• Thus, the actual attendance is $\boxed{75 \text{ percent}}$ of the projected attendance, since:

$$\frac{90}{120} = \frac{3}{4} = 75\%$$

(10) Interest Problems – Every now and then, a GRE problem will involve the concept of interest.

• Such problems tend to be fairly simple but do require a basic understanding of how interest works.

➤ In general, there are two types of interest: simple and compound.

• SIMPLE interest is defined as PRINCIPAL × RATE × TIME. This relationship can be stated with the formula $\boxed{I = PRT}$, in which I = Interest, P = Principal, R = Interest Rate, and T = Times per year:

• "Principal" refers to the amount of money deposited or borrowed, "Rate" to the interest rate, and "Time" to the length of time that the money is deposited or borrowed.

➤ The concept of simple interest is best demonstrated through an example.

• Imagine that Alice had $10,000 in a savings account that paid 10% a year in simple interest. At the end of year 1, the account would be worth $11,000, since 10% of $10,000 = $1,000, and $10,000 + $1,000 = $11,000.

• Likewise, at the end of year 2, the account would be worth $12,000, since 10% of the original $10,000 principal is $1,000 and $11,000 + $1,000 = $12,000.

➤ In other words, **only the original principal generates interest**. The interest earned by the original principal does NOT garner interest.

• To solve simple interest problems, simply **use the $I = PRT$ formula** given above. Plug in what you know and solve for the remaining variable. Consider the following:

If Jack agrees to a 10-year loan of $250 at a simple interest rate of 6 percent per year, how much interest, in dollars, does he owe after 4 years?

(A) 35   (B) 60   (C) 75   (D) 90   (E) 100

Answer. B. If $I = PRT$, then Jack owes $60 in interest after 4 years, since his principal = $250, his rate = 6%, and the time in years = 4 years:

$$I = 25\cancel{0} \times \frac{6}{10\cancel{0}} \times 4 = 5(\cancel{2}) \times \frac{3(\cancel{2})}{\cancel{2}(\cancel{2})} \times 4 = 5(3)(4) = \$60$$

- A second example:

**A 6-percent student loan has a single interest payment of $540 each year.
What is the principal of the loan?**

Quantity A	Quantity B
The total value, in dollars, of the principal	$9,000

Answer: C. If the rate of the loan is 6% and the interest payment is $540 **once a year**, then, according to $I = PRT$:

$$540 = P \times \frac{6}{100} \times 1$$

Thus, principal of the loan is $9,000, as:

$$540 = P \times \frac{6}{100} \times 1 \quad \rightarrow \quad P = 540 \times \frac{100}{6} = \cancel{\times}(90) \times \frac{100}{\cancel{\times}} = 9,000 = P$$

➢ COMPOUND interest, unlike simple interest, is added back to the original principal so that **both the principal and the accrued interest garner interest**.

- For example, a $10,000 saving account that pays 10% interest **compounded annually** would be worth $11,000 after one year, since 10% of $10,000 = $1,000 and $10,000 + $1,000 = $11,000.

- After two years, however, the account would be worth $12,100, since 10% of $11,000 = $1,100 and $11,000 + $1,100 = $12,100.

➢ Most compound interest problems on the GRE are little more than CONSECUTIVE PERCENT problems.

- Their chief difficulty stems from terms such as "annually", "semiannually", or "quarterly". These terms merely indicate how frequently interest is compounded. For example, an account that earns 8% interest:

earns 8% interest ONCE a year	… if it is compound Annually
earns 4% interest TWICE a year	… if it is compound Semiannually
earns 2% interest FOUR times a year	… if it is compound Quarterly

- Consider the following:

A 1-year, $10,000 certificate of deposit pays interest at an annual rate of 6 percent compounded semiannually. What will be the total amount of interest, in dollars, paid on the certificate at maturity?

(A) 600   (B) 609   (C) 900   (D) 10,600   (E) 10,690

Answer: $609. If the certificate pays 6% interest compounded **semiannually**, it pays 3% **twice a year**. Thus, at the end of 6 months, the certificate will generate $300 in interest, as:

$$3\% \text{ of } 10,000 = 1\% \times 3 = \$100 \times 3 = \$300$$

The new principal, therefore, equals the initial $10,000 + $300 of accrued interest. So, at maturity, the certificate will generate an extra $309 in interest, since 3% of $10,300 is $309:

$$3\% \text{ of } 10,300 = 1\% \times 3 = \$103 \times 3 = \$309$$

Thus, the total interest paid will be $609, as $300 + $309 = $609. Remember: in compound interest problems, **the accrued interest earns interest!**

> ➤ **Compound interest** can also be expressed by the following formula, in which P = Principal, R = Interest Rate, T = Times per year, and Y = Years:

$$\text{Total Value} = P(1+\frac{R}{T})^{TY}$$

• It is HIGHLY UNLIKELY that you will ever need to use this formula to calculate interest, since the formula is difficult to use with the GRE's onscreen calculator (it can't perform exponents). Questions can, however, express their answer choices in terms of the formula. In such cases, knowing the formula can be crucial. Consider the following:

If $100 were invested at 8 percent interest compounded quarterly, the total value of the investment, in dollars, at the end of 3 years would be?

(A) $100(1.02)^4$ (B) $100(1.02)^{12}$ (C) $100 + (0.08)^{12}$ (D) $100 + (1.08)^{12}$ (E) $100 + 12(1.02)$

Answer: B. According to the compound interest formula, $100 invested at 8% interest compounded quarterly would equal $100(1.02)^{12}$ at the end of 3 years, since:

$$P\left(1+\frac{R}{T}\right)^{TY} = 100\left(1+\frac{0.08}{4}\right)^{4 \times 3} = 100(1+0.02)^{12} = 100(1.02)^{12}$$

> ➤ On a final note, when working with compound interest, it's worth remembering that the MORE frequent the compounding, the more interest there will be.

• It's also worth remembering that, given the same rate and principal, compound interest will always generate more interest than simple interest.

(11) Alterations – Any percent problem in which a MIXTURE of elements is ALTERED or changed will henceforth be referred to as an alteration problem.

• Alteration problems can always be solved with a **Mixture Table**.

	Original	Change	Total
Element *A*			
Element *B*			
Total			

• **Each row** in a mixture table represents the original amount of an ingredient, its change, and their total. **Each column** adds down to a total as well.

➢ To use a mixture table, simply fill in the quantities that you've been given and add up what you can.

• If you need to compute a percent, **do so before you enter the information into your chart**. To give you a sense of how a Mixture Table works, consider the following:

A bottle is filled to 60 percent of total capacity. If 6 ounces of soda water are added to a mixture that is currently 40 percent orange juice and 60 percent apple juice, causing the bottle to fill to capacity, what percent of the mixture will be orange juice?

(A) 15%   (B) 18%   (C) 20%   (D) 22%   (E) 24%

Answer. E. Since the bottle contains a **mixture** of orange juice and apple juice, to which 6 oz of soda are added, this is an alteration problem.

If the bottle is **originally** filled to 60% capacity, and 6 oz of soda water cause the bottle to fill, then 6 oz = 40% of the bottle's capacity. Thus, 15 oz = 100% of the bottle's capacity, as:

$$\frac{6 \text{ oz}}{40 \text{ percent}} = \frac{x \text{ oz}}{100 \text{ percent}} \quad \rightarrow \quad 600 = 40x \quad \rightarrow \quad \frac{600}{40} = \frac{60}{4} = 15 = x$$

If the bottle's **total** capacity is 15 oz, and 6 oz are soda water, then the **original** 9 oz must be a mixture of 3.6 oz of orange juice and 5.4 oz of apples juice, since 40% of 9 oz = 0.4(9) = 3.6 oz and 60% of 9 oz = 0.6(9) = 5.4 oz.

Thus, if the **final** mixture contains 15 oz, and 3.6 of those ounces are orange juice, the mixture will be 24% orange juice, as:

	Original	Change	Total
Soda	0	+6	6
Orange	3.6		3.6
Apple	5.4		5.4
Total	9	+6	15

$$\frac{3.6}{15} = \frac{36}{150} = \frac{\cancel{6}(6)}{\cancel{6}(25)} = \frac{24}{100} = 24\%$$

➢ In the previous problem, you may have noticed that the mixture table wasn't really necessary.

• It may have been a convenient way of arranging information, but we didn't actually need it to solve the problem. As alteration problems become more DIFFICULT, however, the table often proves crucial to determining relationships.

• Consider the following:

Jeff has a collection of 1,200 stamps, 20 percent of which are Canadian. If 300 stamps are added to the collection, how many of the additional stamps must be Canadian in order to raise the percent of Canadian stamps in the collection to 30 percent?

(A) 120   (B) 150   (C) 180   (D) 210   (E) 240

Answer. D. Since Jeff's stamp collection contains a mix of Canadian and non-Canadian stamps, to which 300 new stamps are added, this is an alteration problem.

If Jeff **originally** has 1,200 stamps, and 20% are Canadian, then 240 of his stamps must be Canadian, since 20% = 10% × 2 = 120(2) = 240. Likewise, if Jeff **adds** 300 stamps to his collection, an unknown number of which are Canadian, he adds x more Canadian stamps and has a **new total** of 1,500.

According to the problem, the percent of Canadian stamps in Jeff's new collection should equal **30 percent of the new total**. Therefore, if Jeff will have a total of 1,500 stamps, exactly 0.3(1,500) of those stamps should be Canadian.

	Original	Change	Total
Canadian	240	$+x$	0.3(1,500)
Other			
Total	1,200	+300	1,500

Our mixture table reveals that 240 + x = 0.3(1,500). Since 30% of 1,500 = 10% × 3 = 150(3) = 450, this equation can be solved as follows:

$$240 + x = 450$$
$$x = 210$$

If x = the additional number of Canadian stamps that Jeff needs to add to his collection, Jeff must add 210 stamps.

• To be sure that you get a proper feel for the Mixture Table, let's look at one last example. This one is a bit more difficult than the previous two:

Last season team *B* won 50 percent of the first 40 games that it played but lost all of its remaining games. If team *B* lost 80 percent of the games that it played, what was the total number of games that team *B* played?

(A) 80   (B) 90   (C) 100   (D) 110   (E) 115

Answer: C. Since team *B*'s first 40 games were a mix of wins and losses, to which an additional number of wins and losses were added, this is an alteration problem.

If team *B* won 50% of its **first** 40 games, it must have won 20 of those games and lost the other 20, since 50% of 40 = 20. Likewise, if team *B* **lost all of its remaining games**, it must have played (and lost) x more games, since the number of remaining games is unknown.

According to the problem, team *B* "lost 80 percent of the games that it played". Therefore, if **team *B* played a total of 40 + x games**, it must have lost 80% of that amount, or $0.8(40 + x)$.

	Original	Change	Total
Wins	20		
Losses	20	$+x$	$0.8(40 + x)$
Total	40	$+x$	$40 + x$

Our mixture table reveals that $20 + x = 0.8(40 + x)$. This equation can be solved as follows:

$$20 + x = 32 + 0.8x$$
$$0.2x = 12$$
$$x = 12/0.2 = 120/2 = 60$$

If team *B* played a total of $40 + x$ games, then it must have played 100 games last season, since $40 + 60 = 100$.

(12) Mixtures – Any percent problem that combines TWO or more MIXTURES will henceforth be referred to as a mixture problem.

• Mixture problems are similar to alteration problems. The sole distinction is that **mixture problems combine separate mixtures**, while alteration problems alter a single mixture.

➢ Like alteration problems, mixture problems can also be solved with a MIXTURE TABLE.

• However, because mixture problems combine multiple mixtures, **the table looks a little different**:

	Mix *A*	Mix *B*	Total
Element *A*			
Element *B*			
Total			

• As before, **each row** in the table represents the amounts of a particular element, but **each column** represents a particular mixture instead of "original" and "change".

➢ This mixture table can be used just like the other. Simply fill in the quantities that you've been given and add up what you can.

• Again, if you need to compute a percent, do so before you enter the information into your chart. Consider the following:

If a 120-ounce solution that is 40 percent chlorine and an 80-ounce solution that is 70 percent chlorine are combined, what percent of the final mixture will be chlorine?

(A) 46% (B) 48% (C) 50% (D) 52% (E) 54%

Answer: D. Since the final mixture is a combination of **separate mixtures**, this is a mixture problem. Solution *A* contains 48 oz of chlorine, as 40% of 120 oz = 10% × 4 = 12(4) = 48. Solution *B* contains 56 oz of chlorine, as 70% of 80 oz = 10% × 7 = 8(7) = 56.

	Sol *A*	Sol *B*	Total
Chlorine	48	56	104
Other			
Total	120	80	200

The **combination** of the two solutions contains 200 oz of solution and 104 oz of chlorine, so the mixture must be 52% chlorine, as:

$$\frac{104}{200} = \frac{52}{100} = 52\%$$

- Here are two more examples for you:

Seed mixture R weighs 100 pounds and is 50 percent millet. Seed mixture S weighs 300 pounds and is x percent millet. If the two mixtures were combined, the resulting mixture would be 20 percent millet. By weight, what percent of mixture S is millet?

(A) 6%   (B) 8%   (C) 10%   (D) 12%   (E) 14%

Answer: C. The final mixture is a combination of **separate mixtures**, so this is a mixture problem. Mixture R contains 50 lb of millet, as 50% of 100 lb = 50 lb. Mixture S contains m lbs of millet, as the amount of millet in the mixture is unknown.

A **combination** of the mixtures would thus weigh a total of 400 lb and contain 80 lb of millet, since 20% of 400 = 0.2(400) = 80.

	Mix R	Mix S	Total
Millet	50	m	80
Other			
Total	100	300	400

Our mixture table reveals that $50 + m = 80$. Since $m = 30$, 10% of mixture S is millet, as:

$$\frac{m}{300} = \frac{30}{300} = 10\%$$

By volume, solution P is 10% iodine and solution Q is 60% iodine. If an unknown quantity of solution P is to be combined with 90 mL of solution Q, and the resulting mixture is 40 percent iodine, how many mL of solution P will be in the mixture?

(A) 50   (B) 60   (C) 70   (D) 80   (E) 90

Answer: B. The final solution is a combination of **separate mixtures**, so this is a mixture problem. Solution P contains $0.1x$ mL of iodine, since 10% of an unknown amount = $0.1(x)$ = $0.1x$. Solution Q contains 54 mL of iodine, since 60% of 90 mL = 10% × 6 = 9(6) = 54.

If 40% of the resulting mixture is iodine, and that mixture contains **a total of x + 90** mL of solution, the resulting mixture must contain 40% of that amount, or **$0.4(x + 90)$** mL of iodine.

	Sol P	Sol Q	Total
Iodine	$0.1x$	54	$0.4(x + 90)$
Other			
Total	x	90	$x + 90$

Our mixture table shows that $0.1x + 54 = 0.4(x + 90)$. This equation can be solved as follows:

$$0.1x + 54 = 0.4x + 36$$
$$18 = 0.3x$$
$$18/0.3 = 180/3 = 60 = x$$

If solution P has a total of x mL of solution, then 60 mL of solution P will be in the mixture.

(13) The Weighted Average Shortcut – In many cases, however, mixture problems DON'T include REAL numbers.

• The easiest way to solve such problems is with a strategy that we like to call the **Weighted Average Shortcut**.

➢ As detailed in our book on <u>Statistics & Data Interpretation</u>, the shortcut is a quick three-step process.

• To start, draw a NUMBER LINE between the percentages of the INDIVIDUAL mixtures.

• For example, if salad dressing *S*, consisting of 50% vinegar, were to be mixed with salad dressing *T*, consisting of 25% vinegar, the mixture of the two dressings could be depicted as follows:

➢ Next, SPLIT the number line into two sections by plotting the percentage of the COMBINED mixture.

• For instance, if the mixture of salad dressings *S* and *T* were to result in a dressing that was 35% vinegar, the 25-space number line above would be split into sections of 10 and 15 spaces, like so:

➢ Once split, **the LONGER section of the number line tells us the percentage of the combined mixture that comes from the "LARGER" mixture**.

• Likewise, the SHORTER section tells us the percentage that comes from the "SMALLER" mixture.

• Here, for example, we know that the LARGER salad dressing represents 60% of the mixture, since the LONGER section spans 15/25, or 3/5, of the number line. Similarly, we know that the SMALLER salad dressing represents 40% of the mixture, since the SHORTER section spans 10/25, or 2/5, of the number line.

- As a LAST step, look back at the number line to see which end of the number line is "pulling" the combined mixture more.

  ➤ **Since a weighted average is essentially a "TUG-OF-WAR", the LARGER of two mixtures will always drag the average CLOSER to itself.**

- In this example, the larger mixture is salad dressing T, since it is winning the tug-of-war. As we can see, the final mixture, at 35%, is closer to point T than to point S:

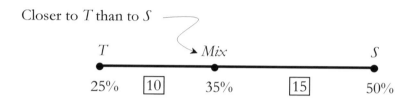

- Thus, we know that 60% of the final mixture comes from salad dressing T, since T is the larger mixture. Likewise, we know that 40% comes from salad dressing S, since S is the smaller mixture.

  ➤ To ensure that you've got the hang of it, let's work through a practice problem together.

- Consider the following:

  By volume, solution A consists of 50 percent iodine and solution B consists of 10 percent iodine. If the two solutions are combined, their resulting mixture is 40 percent iodine. What percent of the final mixture is solution A?

  (A) 25% (B) 33% (C) 40% (D) 67% (E) 75%

- Since this mixture problem involves NO real numbers, it can be solved with the "Weighted Average Shortcut".

  ➤ According to the problem, solution A is 50% iodine, solution B is 10% iodine, and the final mixture is 40% iodine.

- This information can be represented on a 40-space number line, as follows:

- As we can see, **the longer section of the number line has a length of 30**, since the distance from 10% to 40% is 30 spaces. Likewise, the shorter section of the number line has a length of 10, since the distance from 40% to 50% is 10 spaces.

  ➢ The longer section, therefore, represents 75% of the mixture, as it spans 30/40 of the number line.

- Similarly, the shorter section represents 25% of the mixture, as it spans 10/40 of the number line.

- We can also see that **solution A is the larger solution, since point A is WINNING the tug-of-war**: the final mixture, at 40%, is closer to point A than to point B.

  ➢ Solution A, therefore, makes up 75% of the final mixture, since the longer section represents the larger solution.

- Thus, the correct answer is (E).

- If the question had asked us what percentage of the mixture came from solution B, the answer would have been 25%. Solution B is losing the tug-of-war, and the shorter section, which equals 25% of this number line, always refers to the smaller mixture.

Drills and Practice Questions

(14) Drills – Follow the instructions for each of the following sections. When converting to fractions, be sure to reduce your fraction as much as possible.

Convert to Percents

1. $\dfrac{40}{100}$

2. 0.15

3. $\dfrac{60}{125}$

4. $\dfrac{2}{9}$

Convert to Fractions and Decimals

5. 16%

6. 125%

7. 0.50%

8. 1,000%

9. $\dfrac{1}{4}$%

10. x%

Calculate

11. 40% of 30

12. 15% of 90

13. 16% of 350

14. 99% of 420

Solve

15. What percent of 80 is 16?

16. What percent is 50 of 40?

17. 40% of what number is 28?

18. 90 is 15% of what number?

19. By what percent is 30 greater than 18?

20. By what percent is 18 less than 30?

Solutions

1. To convert a fraction to a percent, **multiply it by 100**:

$$\frac{40}{100} \times 100 = 40\%$$

2. To convert a decimal to a percent, multiply it by 100 or **shift the decimal point two spaces to the right**:

$$0.15 = 15\%$$

3. When converting difficult fractions, be sure to **break up the numbers** after multiplying by 100:

$$\frac{60}{125} \times 100 = \frac{60}{5(25)} \times 4(25) = \frac{60}{5} \times 4 = 12 \times 4 = 48\%$$

4. In some cases you may find it easier to convert a fraction to a decimal before you multiply by 100:

$$\frac{2}{9} = 2 \times \frac{1}{9} = 2 \times 0.\bar{1} = 0.\bar{2} \times 100 = 22.\bar{2}\%$$

5. To convert a percent to a fraction, **divide it by 100**. To convert a percent to a decimal, **shift its decimal point** two spaces to the left:

$$16\% = \frac{16}{100} = \frac{4(4)}{4(25)} = \frac{4}{25} \qquad\qquad 16\% = 0.16$$

6. Always **break down numbers** when simplifying fractions:

$$125\% = \frac{125}{100} = \frac{5(25)}{4(25)} = \frac{5}{4} \qquad\qquad 125\% = 1.25$$

7. To convert a percent to a fraction, **divide it by 100**. To convert a percent to a decimal, **shift its decimal point two spaces to the left**:

$$0.50\% = \frac{0.50}{100} = \frac{5}{1,000} = \frac{1}{200} \qquad\qquad 0.50\% = 0.005$$

8. Large percents can be confusing but should be handled just like other percents:

$$1,000\% = \frac{1,000}{100} = 10 \qquad\qquad 1,000\% = 10.00$$

9. Dividing a **fractional percent** will give you a "fraction containing a fraction". To simplify such fractions, be sure to **multiply the top by the "flip" of the bottom**. You can also express the fraction as a decimal before converting it:

$$\frac{1}{4}\% = \frac{\frac{1}{4}}{100} = \frac{1}{4} \times \frac{1}{100} = \frac{1}{400} \qquad \frac{1}{4}\% = 0.25\% = 0.0025$$

10. Variable percents should ONLY be represented as fractions:

$$x\% = \frac{x}{100}$$

11. In most cases, the easiest way to calculate a percent is with the "**10% Shortcut**". Remember, to take 10% of a number, shift its decimal point one space to the left:

$$40\% \text{ of } 30 = 4 \times 10\% = 4 \times 3 = 12$$

12. To take 15% of a number, take 10% and then 5%:

$$15\% \text{ of } 90 \rightarrow 10\% + 5\% = 9 + (\text{half of } 9) = 9 + 4.5 = 13.5$$

13. The "**Fraction Approach**" is very effective with complicated percents. Remember, the word *of* means "multiply":

$$16\% \text{ of } 350 = \frac{16}{100} \times 350 = \frac{16}{10} \times 35 = \frac{2(8)}{2(5)} \times 5(7) = 8(7) = 56$$

14. You can also use the "1% Shortcut" to determine complicated percents. To take 1% of a number, shift its decimal point two spaces to the left:

$$99\% \text{ of } 420 = 100\% - 1\% = 420 - 4.2 = 415.8$$

15. To calculate "part-to-whole relationships", use the proportion **part/whole = percent/100**. Here, the *part* is 16 and the *whole* is 80:

$$\frac{16}{80} = \frac{x}{100} \rightarrow 16(100) = 80x \rightarrow x = \frac{16(100)}{80} = \frac{16(10)}{8} = 2(10) = 20\%$$

16. Sometimes the part is larger than the whole. If you're confused about which value is the "part" and which is the "whole", simply remember that **"is = part"** and **"of = whole"**. Here, *is* = 50 and *of* = 40, so the *part* is 50 and the *whole* is 40:

$$\frac{50}{40} = \frac{x}{100} \rightarrow 50(100) = 40x \rightarrow x = \frac{50(100)}{40} = \frac{5(5)(25)}{5} = 5(25) = 125\%$$

17. The *percent* is 40 and the *part* is 28, so the *whole* is:

$$\frac{28}{x} = \frac{40}{100} \quad \rightarrow \quad 28(100) = 40x \quad \rightarrow \quad x = \frac{28(10\cancel{0})}{4\cancel{0}} = \frac{28(10)}{4} = 7(10) = 70$$

18. The *part* is 90 and the *percent* is 15, so the *whole* is:

$$\frac{90}{x} = \frac{15}{100} \quad \rightarrow \quad 90(100) = 15x \quad \rightarrow \quad x = \frac{90(100)}{15} = \frac{90(100)}{3(5)} = 30(20) = 600$$

19. To solve "percent greater or less than" questions, first place the difference over the **"greater or less than"** amount. Then multiply the result by 100 to convert the fraction into a percent. Here 30 is **"greater than 18"**, so 18 is the "greater than amount":

$$\frac{30 - 18}{18} = \frac{12}{18} = \frac{2}{3} = 0.6\overline{6} \times 100 = 66.\overline{6}\%$$

20. Here 18 is **"less than 30"**, so 30 is the "less than amount":

$$\frac{30 - 18}{30} = \frac{12}{30} = \frac{2(\cancel{6})}{5(\cancel{6})} = 0.4 \times 100 = 40\%$$

(15) Problem Sets – The following questions have been arranged into three groups: fundamental, intermediate, and rare or advanced.

• Whether you're aiming for a perfect score or a score closer to average, mastery of the concepts in the FUNDAMENTAL questions is absolutely essential.

➢ As you might expect, the INTERMEDIATE questions are more difficult but are essential for test-takers who need an above-average score or higher.

• Finally, the RARE or ADVANCED questions test concepts that are very sophisticated or seldom encountered on the GRE. Mastery of such questions is required only if you need a math score above the 90th percentile.

• As always, if you find yourself confused, bogged down with busy work, or stuck, don't be afraid to fall back on your "Plan B" strategies!

Fundamental

$$x > 0$$

Quantity A	Quantity B
0.25% of x	$\frac{1}{4}x$

1.

An antique store purchased identical chairs at a cost of $40 apiece and sold each of them for 30 percent above cost.

Quantity A	Quantity B
The price at which the store sold each chair	$52.00

2.

3.   If membership of a fan club increases from 150 to 180, what is the percent increase?

(A) 16.6%   (B) 18%   (C) 20%   (D) 50%   (E) 60%

Quantity A	Quantity B
48.2 percent of 312	160

4.

Sherpa
Prep

5. A merchant made a profit of $4 on the sale of an umbrella that cost the merchant $12. Approximately what is the profit expressed as a percent of the merchant's cost?

    (A) 33%   (B) 50%   (C) 67%   (D) 200%   (E) 300%

6. If the sales tax on a stereo priced at $250 is between 4 percent and 7 percent, then the cost (price plus sales tax) of the stereo could be which of the following

    Select all possible costs.

    A $250   B $262   C $268   D $276   E $290

    Lisa spent $750 buying a used computer and $270 upgrading it. Then she sold the computer for 30 percent more than the amount she spent buying and upgrading it.

Quantity A	Quantity B

7. The price at which Lisa sold $1,300
    the computer

8. At a local mall, Jack found a jacket that was marked down 40 percent from its regular retail value. If Jack purchased the jacket for $96, what was its presale price, in dollars?

9. From 1950 to 1960, the value of a certain stock increased 40 percent. From 1960 to 1970, its value decreased 40 percent. What was the overall percent change in the value of the stock from 1950 to 1970?

    (A) –16%   (B) –12%   (C) 0   (D) +12%   (E) +16%

Quantity A	Quantity B

10. $1\frac{4}{5}$ percent of 2,500 $3^2 \cdot 5$

11.   70% of what number is 42?

```
┌─────────────────────┐
│                     │
└─────────────────────┘
```

Alan's salary, which is less than $50,000, is 85 percent of Brenda's salary. Connor's salary is 70 percent of Alan's salary.

	Quantity A	Quantity B
12.	Brenda's salary	Connor's salary

A retail shop made a profit of $4.25 on the sale price of a shirt that cost the shop $15.75.

	Quantity A	Quantity B
13.	The profit expressed as a percent of the cost to the retail shop	The profit expressed as a percent of the sale price

14.   At college C, 150 faculty members are male and 200 are female. If 18% of the male faculty members and 12.5% of the female faculty members teach social sciences, approximately what percent of the faculty members teaching social sciences are male?

(A) 38%   (B) 42%   (C) 45%   (D) 46%   (E) 52%

The original price of a sofa was 20 percent less than the sofa's $800 suggested retail price. The price at which the sofa was sold was 20 percent less than the original price.

	Quantity A	Quantity B
15.	The price at which the sofa was sold	40% of the sofa's suggested retail price

16.   Aiden's weekly salary is $30 less than Sophia's weekly salary. If Aiden's weekly salary is $210, then Aiden's weekly salary is what percent less than Sophia's weekly salary, to the nearest 0.1 percent?

(A) 12.5%   (B) 12.9%   (C) 13.4%   (D) 13.8%   (E) 14.3%

Intermediate

17. From 2002 to 2006, the value of a certain stock increased from $200 to $800. By what percent did the value of the stock increase?

(A) 25%   (B) 33%   (C) 200%   (D) 300%   (E) 400%

An increase in the number of computers at Company X to 120 percent of the original amount coincided with the addition of 30 new computer programmers.

Quantity A	Quantity B
18. The percent increase in the number of computer programmers at company X	The percent increase in the number of computers at Company X

Nourah used $630 to buy a mattress. This amount was 15% of her monthly income.

Quantity A	Quantity B
19. The amount of Nourah's earnings last month not used to buy the mattress	$3,570

20. Which of the following is equal to $\frac{1}{8}$ of 0.001 percent?

(A) 1.25×10^{-7} (B) 1.25×10^{-6} (C) 1.25×10^{-5} (D) 1.25×10^{-4} (E) 1.25×10^{-3}

Before a recent demotion, Steve's income was 26 percent more than Tara's. After the demotion, Steve's income was 26 percent less than his old income.

Quantity A	Quantity B
21. Tara's income	Steve's new income

22. In 2008, the value of a certain stock was projected to rise 25%, but actually decreased 50%. What percent of the projected stock value was the actual stock value?

(A) 33%   (B) 40%   (C) 60%   (D) 67%   (E) 75%

23. The value of a $400 ticket is raised by 30 percent and then reduced by x percent. If the final value of the ticket is $364, what is the value of x?

$$\boxed{}$$

The sales tax in state S is 8%.
All group discounts at restaurant R are 15%.
Restaurant R is in state S.

Quantity A	Quantity B

24. The price of a meal at restaurant R if the state tax is applied before the the group discount | The price of the same meal at restaurant R if the group discount is applied before the state tax

25. In 2002, country A's aggregate wheat imports totaled 14 billion dollars and its wheat imports from the United states totaled 5 billion dollars. The value of country A's wheat imports from the United States was approximately what percent less than the value of its aggregate wheat imports?

(A) 35%   (B) 65%   (C) 70%   (D) 120%   (E) 140%

Rare or Advanced

Maria signs a 30-year, $120,000 loan with simple interest computed annually at a rate of 4 percent.

	Quantity A	Quantity B
26.	The amount of interest, in dollars, that Maria owes after 8 months	$3,200

27. The size of a certain town increased by 30 percent between 1980 and 1990, but decreased 40% between 1990 and 2000. If the population of the town was 3,900 in 1990, what was the difference in the town's population between 1980 and 2000?

(A) 660   (B) 1,170   (C) 2,340   (D) 3,000   (E) 3,900

Last year, team X won more games than it lost. This year, the team's wins decreased by the same percent that its losses increased. Team X still won more games than it lost. There were no tie games either year.

	Quantity A	Quantity B
28.	The percent change in the total number of games played by team X from last year to this year	0

29. 40 percent of x is equal to 30 percent of y. If $xy \neq 0$, then x is what percent of y?

(A) 33%   (B) 40%   (C) 55%   (D) 60%   (E) 75%

30. 60 percent of the marbles in a jar are red. Twenty marbles are to be added to the jar, three of which will be red. If 50 percent of its marbles, after the addition, are to be red, how many marbles will the jar hold?

(A) 60   (B) 70   (C) 80   (D) 90   (E) 100

31. Solutions A and B consist of 10 percent and 15 percent malt, respectively. If the two are combined, the resulting mixture is 12.6 percent malt. What percent of the final mixture is solution A?

(A) 46% (B) 48% (C) 50% (D) 52% (E) 54%

32. Positive integer p is 25 percent of 50 percent of positive integer q, and p percent of positive integer q equals 50. What is the value of q?

(A) 100 (B) 160 (C) 200 (D) 250 (E) 400

33. If $m > 0$, $y > 0$, and x is $2m$ percent of $4y$, then, in terms of m, y is what percent of x?

(A) $\dfrac{1,250}{m}$ (B) $\dfrac{7m}{1,000}$ (C) $\dfrac{m}{1,250}$ (D) $\dfrac{2,000}{m}$ (E) $2,500m$

(16) Solutions: Percents – Video solutions for each of the previous questions can be found on our website at **www.sherpaprep.com/videos**.

• BOOKMARK this address for future visits!

 ➢ To view the videos, you'll need the LOGIN and PASSWORD that you created upon registering your copy of Word Problems.

• If you have yet to register your book yet, please go to **www.sherpaprep.com/activate** and enter your email address, last name, and shipping address.

• Be sure to provide the SAME last name and shipping address that you used to purchase your copy of Master Key to the GRE or to enroll in your GRE course with Sherpa Prep!

 ➢ When checking your answers, we encourage you to watch the solution for any problem that you answered INCORRECTLY

• The same goes for any problem that took you MORE than TWO MINUTES to solve.

• After digesting the explanation, REVISIT your mistake a couple of days later to ensure that the problem no longer poses issues to you.

 ➢ If you struggle to solve the problem a SECOND time, add it to your "LOG of ERRORS" and redo it every few weeks.

• Solving tricky questions MORE THAN ONCE is the best way to learn from your mistakes and to avoid similar difficulties on your actual exam.

Fundamental	Intermediate		Rare or Advanced
1. B	11. 60	21. A	26. C
2. C	12. A	22. B	27. A
3. C	13. A	23. 30	28. B
4. B	14. E	24. C	29. E
5. A	15. A	25. B	30. D
6. B	16. A		31. B
7. A	17. D		32. C
8. 160	18. D		33. A
9. A	19. C		
10. C	20. B		

Chapter 3

Algebraic
Word Problems

Algebraic Word Problems

To be discussed:

Fundamental Concepts

Whether you're aiming for a perfect score or a score closer to average, mastery of the following concepts is essential.

Rare or Advanced Concepts

The following concepts are either advanced or are tested only on rare occasions. If you don't need an elite math score, don't waste your time!

Practice Questions & Drills

There's no substitute for elbow grease. Practice your new skills to ensure that you internalize what you've studied.

Fundamental Concepts

(1) Introduction – At its core, an Algebraic Word Problem is an algebra problem that has been expressed with words rather than math symbols.

- Consider a statement such as "some number is three more than two times itself."

  ➤ At first blush, you might not think of it as an algebra equation. But look closely at the words. Many of them are just substitutes for common math operations.

- *More than?* That's another way to say "plus". *Times?* That means "multiply". *Some number?* That's just a variable, such as *x*.

- In fact, we can translate this entire phrase, word-for-word, into the following equation, simply by turning the words into math symbols:

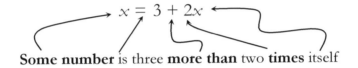

$$x = 3 + 2x$$

Some number is three **more than** two **times** itself

  ➤ Algebraic Word Problems are very common for the GRE.

- In general, roughly 33% of GRE questions are word problems. Of these, approximately 20% tend to be Algebraic Word Problems.

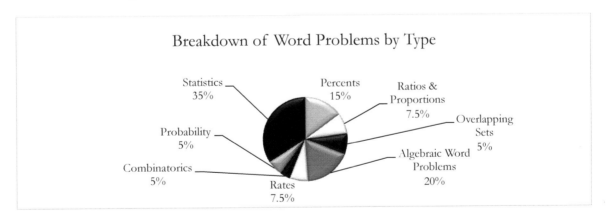

Breakdown of Word Problems by Type

- This may not seem like a lot, but it usually amounts to 3 questions on a typical exam.

- So, work through this section carefully. Even if much of it seems simple or straightforward, the time will be well spent.

(2) Translations – Translations are the simplest type of Algebraic Word Problem.

• As the word "translation" suggests, such problems are literal "word-for-word" renderings of ordinary algebra equations.

> ➤ In order to solve them, you simply need to CONVERT the words back into math symbols.

• When doing so, translate the words in the ORDER that the information is given. **The sequence of your equation should match the sequence of the words.**

• Take the statement "7 more than $5n$ is 4 times the sum of 3 and n." Notice how the order of the translation directly MIRRORS the wording of the statement:

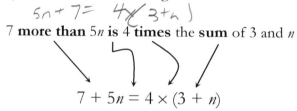

$$7 + 5n = 4 \times (3 + n)$$

> ➤ In other words, "LET the WORDS DO the WORK" should be your guiding principle when solving translations.

• If a problem contains "translation words", don't overthink the information. Just transcribe the information word-for-word.

• To ensure that you've got the basic principle, consider the statement "twice a certain number is half the difference of 5 and itself."

> ➤ As with the previous example, notice how the order of the equation directly MIRRORS the wording of the statement:

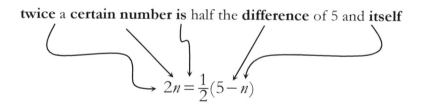

$$2n = \frac{1}{2}(5 - n)$$

• If you're UNSURE whether your translation is correct, TEST the solution. If the solution satisfies your equation, your work should be correct. For example, the solution to the equation above is $n = 1$. Since $2(1) = \frac{1}{2}(5-1)$, our translation should be correct.

Sherpa
Prep

➢ Translations are easy to recognize, since they are generally littered with words that stand for math symbols.

• Similarly, the mathematical equivalents of most "translation words" are usually self-evident. Hence, *sum* means "add", *decrease by* means "subtract", and *product* means "multiply".

• Some words or phrases, however, may not be obvious to you. If any of the following are not obvious, be sure to MEMORIZE them.

ADDITION	add to, sum, plus, more than, older than, total, farther than, greater than, and, increase by, exceed
SUBTRACTION	subtract, difference, minus, less than, younger than, fewer than, decrease by, lose, in excess, beyond
MULTIPLICATION	multiply by, of, by, at, times, product, twice, double, triple, thrice, etc.
DIVISION	per, goes into, percent, in, divisible by, out of, for every, quotient, divisor, the ratio of x to y
EQUAL SIGN	is, was, has, will be, had, equals, goes for, costs, adds up to, weighs, totals to
VARIABLE	what, a certain number, some number, how many, how much, some group

➢ A few words that many test-takers find difficult to translate are *AT, BEYOND,* and *IN EXCESS OF.*

• As you can see from the list above, the word *at* means "multiply". Thus, we would translate the statement "*n* pounds of meat at *p* dollars a pound costs 15 dollars", as:

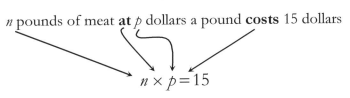

$$n \times p = 15$$

- Similarly, the phrase _in excess of_ means "subtract". Thus, we would translate the statement "8 percent of sales in excess of 5,000 dollars", as:

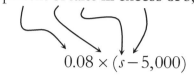

$$0.08 \times (s - 5,000)$$

- Since the word _beyond_ also means "subtract", the statement "8 percent of sales beyond 5,000 dollars" would be translated the same way.

> ➤ Finally, when assigning variables to unknown elements, always **choose MEANINGFUL variables**.

- For example, let boys = b and girls = g. Likewise, let sales = s and costs = c. Assigning x and y can lead to careless mistakes.

- Take the statement "the smaller number is $\frac{3}{5}$ of the larger." If you let small = x and large = y, the two numbers become easy to confuse, since x does not intuitively signify a smaller number.

> ➤ However, if you were to translate the statement with meaningful variables, the two numbers are unlikely to be confused.

- Here, s clearly signifies "small" and l clearly signifies "large":

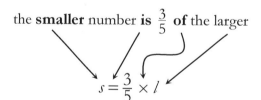

$$s = \frac{3}{5} \times l$$

(3) Percents – In our discussion of Percents, we pointed out that percent problems comparing a part to a whole can be solved with the following proportion:

$$\frac{\text{Part}}{\text{Whole}} = \frac{\text{"Percent"}}{100}$$

• For example, to determine "what percent of 250 is 45", we can set up the following relationship, since we know the **part** and the **whole**, but not the **percent**:

$$\text{part} \qquad \text{"percent"}$$
$$\frac{45}{250} = \frac{x}{100}$$
$$\text{whole}$$

➤ Since the word *percent* means "divided by 100", such problems can also be solved as TRANSLATIONS.

• For example, the question "what percent of 250 is 45" can be translated as:

$$\textbf{what} \text{ percent } \textbf{of } 250 \textbf{ is } 45$$
$$\frac{x}{100} \times 250 = 45$$

• Hence, 45 is 18 percent of 250, since dividing both sides of the equation by 250 gives us:

$$\frac{x}{100} = \frac{45}{250} \quad \rightarrow \quad x = \frac{45}{25\cancel{0}} \cdot 10\cancel{0} \quad \rightarrow \quad x = \frac{9(\cancel{5})}{\cancel{5}(\cancel{5})} \cdot 2(\cancel{5}) = 18$$

➤ In many cases, you may find it equally easy to solve percent problems with EITHER technique.

• There are problems, however, that are more conveniently solved as translations. Take the statement "35 percent of *n* percent of 4,800 is 12".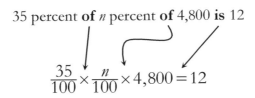

• Solving it with the proportion above would be difficult. Translating it as follows isn't:

$$35 \text{ percent } \textbf{of } n \text{ percent } \textbf{of } 4{,}800 \textbf{ is } 12$$
$$\frac{35}{100} \times \frac{n}{100} \times 4{,}800 = 12$$

> ➤ **We encourage you to learn BOTH strategies.** Knowing both will allow you to solve problems in which your preferred strategy may be difficult to use.

• To get a better feel for "translating percents", consider the following:

$$\frac{n}{100} \cdot 20 = 6 + (-n)$$

n percent of 20 is 6 more than $-n$.

Quantity A		**Quantity B**
$n - 5$		0

Answer. C. To solve for n, we can translate the statement as follows:

n percent of 20 is 6 more than $-n$

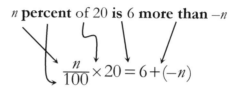

$$\frac{n}{100} \times 20 = 6 + (-n)$$

The left side of this equation can be reduced to $\frac{n}{100} \times 20 = \frac{20n}{100} = \frac{n}{5}$. Thus, $n = 5$, since:

$$\frac{n}{5} = 6 + (-n) \quad \rightarrow \quad n = 30 - 5n \quad \rightarrow \quad 6n = 30$$

If $n = 5$, then $n - 5 = 0$, since $5 - 5 = 0$. Therefore, the two quantities must be equal.

• A second example:

$$\frac{7xy}{100}$$

$$\frac{x}{100} \circ \frac{y}{100} \cdot 7$$

x and y are positive integers.

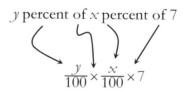

Quantity A	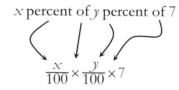	**Quantity B**
x percent of y percent of 7		y percent of x percent of 7

Answer. C. The two quantities can be translated as follows:

x percent of y percent of 7

$$\frac{x}{100} \times \frac{y}{100} \times 7$$

y percent of x percent of 7

$$\frac{y}{100} \times \frac{x}{100} \times 7$$

Thus, the two quantities must be equal, since:

$$\frac{x}{100} \times \frac{y}{100} \times 7 = \frac{7xy}{10,000} \qquad\qquad \frac{y}{100} \times \frac{x}{100} \times 7 = \frac{7xy}{10,000}$$

(4) Tricky Translations – As we've seen, Translations can be solved by transcribing their words in the order that they've been written.

• There are, however, several phrases that violate this principle.

➤ The most important of these phrases are LESS THAN, YOUNGER THAN, and FEWER THAN.

• If one term is "some amount" less than another, that amount must be SUBTRACTED from the SECOND term. Take the statement "x is 3 less than y." Given the order of the words, you might be tempted to write this equation as follows:

x **is 3 less than** y

$$x = 3 - y \qquad \longleftarrow \qquad \text{Mistake!}$$

• Unfortunately, doing so would be a mistake. To transcribe this equation properly, we need to subtract 3 from the second term:

x **is 3 less than** y

$$x = y - 3 \qquad \longleftarrow \qquad \text{Correct!}$$

➤ Phrases such as LESS THAN and GREATER THAN can also be tricky when used with FRACTIONS.

• Take the statement "x is 1/3 greater than y." Given the order of the words, you might be tempted to write the following:

x **is 1/3 greater than** y

$$x = \frac{1}{3} + y \qquad \longleftarrow \qquad \text{Mistake!}$$

• Such a phrase, however, indicates that x equals a value of y that is 1/3 greater than its CURRENT size. Since $y + \frac{1}{3}y = \frac{4}{3}y$:

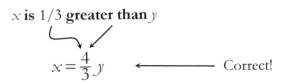

x **is 1/3 greater than** y

$$x = \frac{4}{3}y \qquad \longleftarrow \qquad \text{Correct!}$$

➢ Finally, watch out for phrases such as AS MANY AS and AS LARGE AS. Such phrases can be very deceptive.

• Take the statement "there are twice as many cats as dogs." Since the word "twice" is next to the word "cats", you might be tempted to translate it as:

twice as many **cats** as dogs

$$2c = d \qquad \longleftarrow \qquad \text{Mistake!}$$

• However, this is wrong. To understand why, imagine that there are 4 cats. If we plug 4 cats into $2c = d$, we get 8 dogs, giving us more dogs than cats! Since the statement indicates that there are more cats than dogs, the correct translation is actually:

twice as many cats as **dogs**

$$c = 2d \qquad \longleftarrow \qquad \text{Correct!}$$

➢ When translating expressions such as AS MANY AS or AS MUCH AS, always MULTIPLY the term after the SECOND "AS".

• In the statement "there are twice as many cats AS dogs", the term after the second "as" is dogs. Likewise, in the statement "Maia earns half as much AS Nancy", the term after the second "as" is Nancy.

• Thus, the correct translation for each statement is:

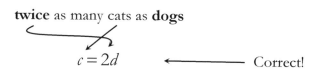

there are **twice** as many cats AS dogs $\qquad$ Maia earns **half** as much AS Nancy

$$c = 2d \qquad\qquad\qquad m = \frac{1}{2}n$$

➢ If you're ever in doubt about how to set up a "Tricky Translation", you can always TEST your translation with numbers.

• We like to call such tests "sanity checks", since a proper translation always matches the meaning of its statement. Take the statement "Al weighs 1/3 less than Bo". The translation $a = b - \frac{1}{3}$ is wrong, since it implies that Al weighs $89\frac{2}{3}$ pounds if Bo weighs 90.

• Since $b - \frac{1}{3}b = \frac{2}{3}b$, the correct translation is $a = \frac{2}{3}b$. We know it's correct because it implies that Al would weigh 60 pounds if Bo weighed 90.

(5) Inequalities – Inequalities can also be expressed with words.

• Take the time to familiarize yourself with the following "translation words". If a phrase is not obvious or familiar to you, commit it to memory.

GREATER Than	$>$	greater than, older than, more than, bigger than
LESS Than	$<$	less than, fewer than, younger than, smaller than,
GREATER Than or EQUAL	$\geq$	greater than or equal to, at least, a minimum of, no less than
LESS Than or EQUAL	$\leq$	less than or equal to, at most, a maximum of, no more than

• When translating inequalities, let the WORDS DO the WORK. As with equations, transcribe the words in the order they're written:

"The sum of five and some number is less than three."

$$5 + x < 3$$

"John has at least $7 more than Bill."

$$j \geq 7 + b$$

"If Cara were to lose $5, she would have no more than 20."

$$c - 5 \leq 20$$

➢ But be careful with the phrases LESS THAN and GREATER THAN. Such phrases have TWO uses.

• If "x is less than y", you have an inequality. If "x is SOME AMOUNT less than y", you have an equation:

INEQUALITY

"Alice is younger than Betty."

$$a < b$$

"Greg's salary is larger than Kevin's."

$$g > k$$

EQUATION

"Alice is 4 years younger than Betty."

$$a = b - 4$$

"Greg's salary is $100 larger than Kevin's."

$$g = 100 + k$$

(6) Stories – Sometimes Translations come with little stories.

- Naturally, we call such problems "Stories".

  ➢ In general, Stories are more difficult than Translations, since they are harder to decipher.

- Unlike Translations, which are littered with obvious "translation words", Stories often HIDE their equations by implying them or stating them indirectly.

- At the heart of every Story, though, is at least one Translation. And, thankfully, in many cases that Translation is somewhat obvious.

  ➢ To get a feel for the difference between a Story and a Translation, consider the following:

A recent delivery increased the amount of grain stored in a certain silo from 16 to 24 metric tons. If the delivery increased the amount of grain in the silo to 60 percent of total capacity, how many metric tons of grain could the silo hold if its total capacity were 150 percent greater?

(A) 40   (B) 60   (C) 80   (D) 84   (E) 100

- When solving a problem like the one above, you may NOT initially recognize that it contains a Translation. That's part of what makes Stories challenging.

- In fact, many test-takers respond to such problems by asking "where do I even start?" And it's a fair question. There are a number of challenges to solving Stories, especially if math doesn't come easily to you.

  ➢ To start, **DON'T try to solve the problem all at once.** This is a common mistake on the part of many test-takers.

- It's usually quite difficult, if not impossible, to solve a Story immediately upon reading it. On the contrary, Stories are more like murder mysteries. There's usually a lot of clues, but it generally takes some sleuthing to see how they fit together.

- It also helps to READ CAREFULLY. Some Stories contain a lot of information, so time can be a challenge. A mistaken assumption or a misreading can result in a good deal of wasted time.

➤ **As you read, TAKE NOTES.** Taking notes can greatly reduce the amount of time spent rereading a problem.

• When doing so, CHOOSE MEANINGFUL VARIABLES to represent things you don't know. For example, in the problem above, we don't know the **capacity** of the silo, so we might write:

$$c = ?$$

• We do know, however, that there were 16 tons of grain **before** the delivery and 24 metric tons **after**, so we might also write:

$$b = 16 \;\rightarrow\; a = 24$$

➤ **If necessary, DRAW PICTURES.** Sometimes the easiest way to recognize relationships is to see them.

• In the problem, for example, we have a silo that contains 24 tons of grain and is 60% full, so we could draw something like:

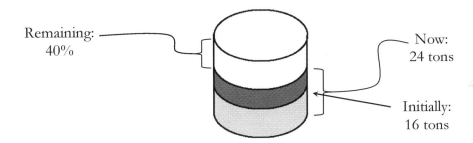

➤ **WRITE DOWN the specific piece of information that the problem is asking for**, and consider what might be necessary to attain it.

• For example, in the problem above, the question asks "how many tons of grain could the silo hold if its total capacity were 150 percent greater?"

• How might we get this information? Well, if we could determine the current capacity of the silo, determining an amount 150 percent greater would simply be a matter of taking 150 percent of the current capacity and adding it to the current total. Thus, we might write down something like:

$$c = ? \;\rightarrow\; \uparrow 150\% \, c = ?$$

➢ After you've taken notes and drawn pictures, **try to ESTABLISH an EQUATION**.

• In some cases this will be easy. Many stories contain obvious Translations that can be transcribed word-for-word. For example, if a problem states that class C has "one more junior than twice the number of seniors", then it clearly contains the following equation:

"the number of juniors is one more than twice the number of seniors"

$$j = 1 + 2s$$

• Sometimes, however, you may not be sure how to express the information that you've been given as an equation. If this is the case, start by looking for any sort of relationship that the problem states or implies.

➢ Often times, you may find that you're **PARTIALLY AWARE** of one or more relationships already.

• For example, in the problem above, you may have noticed yourself thinking something like:

"There are 24 tons in the silo when the silo is at 60% of capacity."

• If you get this far, see whether you can **boil the relationship down to a partial equation using a combination of words and math**. In the case above, for example, you might think or write down something like the following:

"24 tons = 60% of capacity"

➢ If you can get to a partial equation, you may find that you can often translate it into a mathematical expression.

• For example, our statement can be translated as follows:

"24 tons = 60% of capacity"

$$24 = \frac{60}{100} \times c$$

• Thus, we know that capacity of the silo is 40, since:

$$24 = \frac{60}{100} \times c \;\; \rightarrow \;\; 24 \times \frac{100}{60} = c \;\; \rightarrow \;\; 4(\cancel{6}) \times \frac{10(\cancel{10})}{\cancel{6}(\cancel{10})} = 4 \times 10 = c$$

> Once you have solved for the variables, **LOOK BACK at the problem** to ensure that you have answered the RIGHT question.

• Story questions often ask you to consider one LAST wrinkle, especially after the difficult portion of the problem has been dealt with.

• For example, in the problem above, the question asks for a capacity that is "150% greater". So far, we've only determined the current capacity. To get the enlarged capacity, we need to take 150% of the current capacity, which is 40, and add it to the current capacity:

$$\text{"150\% of } c + \text{ original } c = \text{?"}$$

$$\left(\frac{150}{100} \times 40\right) + 40 \quad \rightarrow \quad \left(\frac{15\cancel{0}}{1\cancel{00}} \times 4\cancel{0}\right) + 40 \quad \rightarrow \quad (15 \times 4) + 40 = 100$$

> Lastly, take a moment to **be sure that your answer MAKES SENSE**. Sometimes, a quick double check will expose a careless error.

• For example, in the problem under consideration, you know that 24 = 60% of the current capacity. Thus, you might ask yourself:

"If 24 is 60% of capacity, does 40 make sense as 100% of capacity?"

• If so, you might further ask:

"If 40 is the original capacity, does 100 makes sense
as a capacity that is 150% greater?"

• If the answer to these questions is "yes", then you're done. However, if the numbers do not seem right, you should reconsider your work. Here, 40 and 100 both make sense, so it's safe to conclude that the answer is 100.

> If this seems like a lot of work, don't be misled. Most of this activity is mental and can be done in a matter of seconds.

• **Writing down the question, taking notes, assigning variables, drawing pictures**: you can do these as you read. **Looking back** to ensure that you've solved the right question and **checking whether your answer makes sense?** These too are quick mental investments.

• **Establishing equations** is always the tough part, but in most cases **the equations you need will be Translations** within the Story, and hence part of your notes, or else implied by your drawing or a key word in the question.

- Let's work through a second example:

Amy rents a car for \$25 plus \$0.35 for every mile driven. Wally rents a car for \$40 plus \$0.20 for every mile driven. How many miles does each have to drive for their respective rentals to cost exactly the same amount?

(A) 65 (B) 85 (C) 100 (D) 110 (E) 120

Answer: C. To start, let's **assign variables** to the things we don't know. Here, there are three unknowns: a = Amy's rental costs, w = Wally's rental costs, and m = their mileage.

Next, let's **take notes** on what we've been told. According to the problem, "Amy rents a car for \$25 plus \$0.35 for every mile driven" and "Wally rents a car for \$40 plus \$0.20 for every mile driven". Since each of these statements is a Translation, we can **establish the following equations**:

"Amy rents for \$25 plus \$0.35 per mile"   "Wally rents for \$40 plus \$0.20 per mile"

$$a = 25 + 0.35m$$ $$w = 40 + 0.20m$$

The next step is the most difficult. We need to find some way to use this information to solve the question. **The clue** is the last part of the question: "How many miles does each have to drive for their respective rentals to cost exactly the **same** amount?"

This statement **implies** that at some point their costs are EQUAL. Thus, we can set their costs equal to determine the mileage:

$$\text{Amy's costs} = \text{Wally's costs}$$
$$25 + 0.35m = 40 + 0.20m$$

Thus, m = 100, since:

$$25 + 0.35m = 40 + 0.20m \quad \rightarrow \quad 0.15m = 15 \quad \rightarrow \quad m = \frac{15}{0.15} = \frac{1{,}500}{15} = 100$$

As a final step, let's quickly **check whether our answer makes sense**. If Amy were to drive 100 miles, she'd pay \$25 + 35% of that distance, in dollars. Since 35% of 100 is 35, she'd pay \$25 + \$35 = \$60.

If Wally were to drive 100 miles, he'd pay \$40 + 20% of that distance, in dollars. Since 20% of 100 is 20, he'd pay \$40 + \$20 = \$60.

Since our work and calculations appear to be accurate, the answer should be (C).

(7) Age Problems – On the surface, Age problems are like any other Story problem.

• In fact, they often seem easier than most, since they're primarily composed of a few basic Translations and little else. Despite this, most test-takers get them wrong.

> ➤ Age problems contain a tricky WRINKLE that's easy to miss. Fortunately, the wrinkle is easy to master.

• When solving age problems, you have to remember that **BOTH PEOPLE MUST AGE**.

• Take the statement "4 years ago, Anna was twice as old as Belle." If we translate it word-for-word, we get:

"4 years ago, Anna was twice as old as Belle."

$$a - 4 = 2b \qquad \longleftarrow \qquad \text{Mistake!}$$

> ➤ This is a MISTAKE. Although the phrase "4 years ago" only appears next to Anne, it ALSO applies to Belle.

• Since both people must age, the CORRECT translation is: 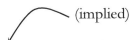 (implied)

"4 years ago, Anna was twice as old as Belle (back then)."

$$a - 4 = 2(b - 4) \qquad \longleftarrow \qquad \text{Correct!}$$

• Notice that we write $2(b - 4)$, and not $2b - 4$, since the statement $2b - 4$ would indicate that Belle is ALWAYS 4 years younger than twice Belle's age.

> ➤ Likewise, take the statement "five years from now, Renee will be 3 years younger than Steve."

• Notice how BOTH PEOPLE age in the correct translation:

MISTAKE	CORRECT
"five years from now, Renee will be 3 years younger than Steve."	"five years from now, Renee will be 3 years younger than Steve (will be)."
$r + 5 = s - 3$	$r + 5 = (s + 5) - 3$

(implied)

• Let's take a look at a couple of Age problems:

Fred is now 9 years older than Jeff. If in 8 years Fred will be twice as old as Jeff, how old will Fred be in 4 years?

(A) 10 (B) 11 (C) 14 (D) 15 (E) 18

Answer. C. Fred is currently 9 years older than Jeff, so we know that $f = 9 + j$. In 8 years, Fred will be twice as old as Jeff. Since both parties will be 8 years older, we also know that:

"Fred in 8 years will be twice as old as Jeff"

$$f + 8 = 2(j + 8)$$

If we **plug** $f = 9 + j$ into $f + 8 = 2(j + 8)$, we get:

$$(9 + j) + 8 = 2(j + 8) \quad \rightarrow \quad j + 17 = 2j + 16 \quad \rightarrow \quad j = 1$$

Since $j = 1$ and $f = 9 + j$, then Fred is currently 10 years old, as $9 + 1 = 10$. Thus, Fred will be 14 years old in 4 years.

- A second example:

Currently, Alex is 12 years older than Sandra. 6 years ago, Alex was three times as old as Sandra. How old was Sandra 2 years ago?

(A) 6 (B) 10 (C) 12 (D) 20 (E) 22

Answer. B. Alex is currently 12 years older than Sandra, so we know that $a = 12 + s$. 6 years ago, Alex was three times as old as Sandra. Since both parties were 4 years older, we also know that:

"6 years ago, Alex was three times as old as Sandra"

$$a - 6 = 3(s - 6)$$

If we **plug** $a = 12 + s$ into $a - 6 = 3(s - 6)$, we get:

$$(12 + s) - 6 = 3(s - 6) \quad \rightarrow \quad s + 6 = 3s - 18 \quad \rightarrow \quad 24 = 2s$$

Since $s = 12$, then Sandra was 10 years old 2 years ago.

(8) Quantity Mixtures – Quantity Mixture problems are easy to spot. They always feature a mix of objects, each with their own cost or value

- For example, a grocer might buy apples for $2 and bananas for $3, or a play might sell adult tickets for $8 and junior tickets for half that amount.

  ➤ An easy way to solve such problems is with the formula below. Naturally, we call it the "Quantity Mixture Formula".

$$\text{Rate}_1 \times \text{Quantity}_1 + \text{Rate}_2 \times \text{Quantity}_2 = \text{Total Cost}$$

- Imagine you were told that a customer purchased small towels for $3 and large towels for $5 and, in doing so, bought 14 towels for a total of $60.

- You could use the formula to set up the following equation:

"$3 small towels and $5 large towels for a total of $60"

$$3s + 5l = 60$$

  ➤ Likewise, if the consumer bought a total of 14 towels, you could also establish the equation $s + l = 14$.

- Finally, if you triple the bottom equation from $s + l = 14$ to $3s + 3l = 42$, you can subtract the two equations as follows to solve for s and l:

$$
\begin{array}{r}
3s + 5l = 60 \\
- \quad 3s + 3l = 42 \\
\hline
2l = 18 \ \rightarrow \ l = 9
\end{array}
$$

- Since $l = 9$ and $s + l = 14$, we know that $s = 5$. Thus, the consumer purchased 5 small towels and 9 large towels.

  ➤ In general, Quantity Mixture problems contain TWO equations, as in the example above.

- To solve for the variables within them, you will need to combine the equations.

- When doing so, we strongly encourage you to use the ELIMINATION strategy we covered in our book on Number Properties & Algebra. With Quantity Mixture problems, elimination is almost always the FASTER strategy.

- Consider the following:

A certain grocery store sells only two types of apples: Fujis and Pippens. Fujis sell for $2 an apple and Pippens sell for $3 an apple. If Wendy purchases 12 apples at that store and pays a total of $27, how many Pippens does Wendy purchase?

(A) 3   (B) 4   (C) 5   (D) 8   (E) 9

Answer: A. Since Fujis have a rate of $2 an apple, Pippens have a rate of $3 an apple, and Wendy spends $27 buying apples, we can set up the following equation:

$$2f + 3p = 27$$

Further, since Wendy buys a total of 12 apples, but only buys Fujis and Pippens, we know that $f + p = 12$. If we double this equation to $2f + 2p = 24$, we can subtract the two equations as follows:

$$2f + 3p = 27$$
$$- \ 2f + 2p = 24$$
$$p = 3$$

Thus, the correct answer must be (A), since $p = 3$.

- A second example for you:

The cost of tickets for a certain play is $4.00 for adults and $3.00 for children. 80 tickets were sold and $310 was collected. How many tickets were sold to children?

(A) 8   (B) 10   (C) 38   (D) 70   (E) 72

Answer: B. Since tickets for adults are $4, tickets for children are $3, and $310 was collected, we can set up the following equation:

$$4a + 3c = 310$$

Further, if 80 tickets were sold, we know that $a + c = 80$. If we quadruple this equation to $4a + 4c = 320$, we can subtract the two equations as follows:

$$4a + 3c = 310$$
$$- \ 4a + 4c = 320$$
$$-c = -10$$

If $-c = -10$, then $c = 10$. Thus, (B) is the correct answer.

(9) FUQ's – In our book on Arithmetic & "Plan B" Strategies, we introduced a type of problem that we like to call "FUQ's".

- As you may recall, the term "FUQ" stands for "Fractions with Unspecified Quantities".

  ➢ In those discussions, we suggested that the key to solving such problems is to PICK NUMBERS.

- Specifically, we recommended that you pick the PRODUCT of the DENOMINATORS to solve them.

- Although many sorts of problems can be FUQ's, most FUQ's are Algebraic Word Problems. Consider the following:

Kennel _K_ has four types of animals. There are 2/3 as many cats as dogs, 1/2 as many ferrets as cats, and 3/4 as many hamsters as ferrets.

Quantity A	**Quantity B**
The fraction of animals in kennel _K_ that is either a cat or a ferret	5/11

Answer: B. Because this problem has fractional quantities but NO concrete values, **let's set the number of dogs equal to 24**, which is the product of the problem's denominators: $3 \times 2 \times 4 = 24$.

If the kennel has "2/3 as many cats as dogs", then it has 16 cats, since 2/3 of 24 = 16. Likewise, if the kennel has "1/2 as many ferrets as cats", then it has 8 ferrets, since 1/2 of 16 = 8. Finally, if the kennel has "3/4 as many as hamsters as ferrets", then it has 6 hamsters, since 3/4 of 8 = 6.

If there are 24 dogs, 16 cats, 8 ferrets, and 6 hamsters, there are 54 animals in the kennel, as 24 + 16 + 8 + 6 = 54. And if 16 of those animals are cats and 8 are ferrets, then 24 of the 54 animals are either a cat or a ferret. Thus, Quantity A = 4/9, since 24/54 = 4/9.

According to the Comparison Trick, 5/11 must be a larger fraction that 4/9, since 45 is greater than 44. Thus, the correct answer is (B), since Quantity B is larger than Quantity A:

$$44 \qquad 45$$
$$\frac{4}{9} \diagdown\!\!\!\!\diagup \frac{5}{11}$$

> ➤ But remember: if your question involves CONCRETE numbers, you CAN'T pick numbers.

- FUQ's never contain real numbers. If you pick numbers for a problem with real numbers, you will likely contradict the information given in the problem.

- Consider the following:

If 1/2 of the marbles in a certain bag are blue, 1/4 are green, 1/5 are red, and the remaining 30 are black, how many marbles does the bag contain?

(A) 240   (B) 310   (C) 450   (D) 510   (E) 600

Answer. E. Since the number of marbles in the bag is unspecified, and the problem contains the fractions 1/2, 1/4 and 1/5, it is tempting to let the number of marbles be $2 \times 4 \times 5 = 40$.

Doing so, however, would be a mistake. According to the problem, there are 30 black marbles in the bag. If the bag were to have 40 marbles, and half were to be blue, then it would be impossible for the bag to have 30 black marbles as well.

Since this problem contains the number 30, we CANNOT pick numbers. Instead, we have to assign variables. Let m = the total number of marbles in the bag. If 1/2 of these marbles are blue, 1/4 are green, and 1/5 are red, then:

$$b = \frac{1}{2}m \qquad g = \frac{1}{4}m \qquad r = \frac{1}{5}m$$

Further, if the collection of marbles equals the sum of the blue, green, red, and black marbles, then:

$$m = \frac{1}{2}m + \frac{1}{4}m + \frac{1}{5}m + 30$$

If we use the "Denominator Trick" to multiply the ENTIRE equation by 20, we get:

$$20 \cdot m = 20 \cdot \frac{1}{2}m + 20 \cdot \frac{1}{4}m + 20 \cdot \frac{1}{5}m + 20 \cdot 30$$
$$20m = 10m + 5m + 4m + 600$$
$$20m = 19m + 600$$
$$m = 600$$

Thus, the bag contains 600 marbles.

(10) Asswholes – In our book on <u>Arithmetic & "Plan B" Strategies</u>, we also introduced a type of problem that we like to call "Asswholes".

- As you may recall, Asswholes contain VARIABLES in the ANSWER choices.

  ➢ In most cases, the easiest way to solve such problems is to ASSIGN whole numbers to variables WITHIN the question.

- To do so, first REPLACE any variables in the problem by picking numbers. Then solve the problem using those numbers.

- Once you've solved the problem, PLUG the values you've picked into the answer choices to see which answer MATCHES your solution.

  ➢ When choosing numbers, it's important that you choose numbers that are EASY to work with and work well together.

- It's also important you OBEY a small set of rules.

- Exam-makers are aware that some test-takers pick numbers, and occasionally design answer choices to foil commonly chosen numbers.

  ➢ Obeying the following rules will help you avoid certain traps that exam-makers build into certain problems:

  ☑ Do not pick the same number more than once.
  ☑ Avoid numbers you see in the question or in the answer choices.
  ☑ Stay away from 0, 1, and 100.

- In other words, if you have to choose values for two variables, do NOT pick the same number for both. And if you see the number 5 in the question or the number 10 in the answer choices, don't pick 5 or 10.

  ➢ Finally, when plugging numbers into the answer choices, try answer choice (A) first. If (A) doesn't work, try (E) next.

- As with "Which of the Following Questions", the correct answer to Asswhole problems is frequently (A) or (E).

- Trying (A) and then (E) may save you time.

> ➤ Although many sorts of problems can be Asswholes, many Asswholes are Algebraic Word Problems.

- In fact, many of the more difficult Algebraic Word Problems happen to be Asswholes. Fortunately, such problems are easily solved with this strategy.

- Consider the following:

A video-conferencing program charges $1.00 for the first 3 minutes and $0.20 for each additional minute. If x is an integer greater than 3, a video-conference x minutes long will cost how many <u>dollars</u>?

$$\text{(A) } \frac{2x}{5} \quad \text{(B) } \frac{x}{5}-2 \quad \text{(C) } \frac{x-5}{3} \quad \text{(D) } \frac{x}{5}+3 \quad \text{(E) } \frac{x+2}{5}$$

- To start, let's pick a value for x. Any value will do, but it's always best to work with small, simple numbers. But we have to **respect the constraints within the problem**.

> ➤ According to the problem, x is "an integer greater than 3", so any value that we pick for x must be a whole number greater than 3.

- Since 4 is the smallest integer greater than the 3, let's make $x = 4$.

- If the conference is 4-minutes long, it should cost $1 for the first 3 minutes and $0.20 for the final minute. Thus, the total cost of the call, in dollars, should be $1.20

> ➤ To finish the problem, we only have to **plug $x = 4$ into the answer choices to see which of them equals $1.20**.

- Let's start with (A). (A) is not the correct answer since it does not equal 1.2:

$$\text{(A) } \frac{2x}{5} \quad \longrightarrow \quad \frac{2(4)}{5} = \frac{8}{5} = 1\frac{3}{5} = \boxed{1.6}$$

- Next, let's test (E). Since (E) does equal 1.2, it is the correct answer.

$$\text{(E) } \frac{x+2}{5} \quad \longrightarrow \quad \frac{4+2}{5} = \frac{6}{5} = 1\frac{1}{5} = \boxed{1.2}$$

- We could test out the remaining answer choices, but there's no need: we've already found the correct answer.

➢ If you were able to solve the previous problem algebraically: great! We still encourage you to incorporate the Asswhole strategy into your "bag of tricks".

• There are plenty of Asswholes more difficult than the last example, and the flexibility to solve a problem in multiple ways can only improve your chances for success.

• A second example:

A grocer has x crates, each containing 9 apples. After selling k apples to each of her customers, the grocer has t apples left over. Which of the following represents the number of customers to which the grocer sold apples?

$$\text{(A) } \frac{9x-t}{k} \quad \text{(B) } \frac{9x+t}{k} \quad \text{(C) } \frac{9x}{k}-t \quad \text{(D) } \frac{9k-t}{x} \quad \text{(E) } \frac{9k+t}{x}$$

• To start, let's pick a value for x. Any value will do, but it's always best to work with small, simple numbers.

➢ Let's make $x = 10$, since 10 is easy to work with. If the grocer has 10 crates with 9 apples each, she therefore has 90 apples.

• Next, let's pick a value for k. The problem says the grocer has "apples left over", so we have to choose a number that will give us a remainder. Let's make $k = 11$.

• If the grocer sells 11 apples to each customer, then **she has 8 customers and 2 apples left over**, since $90 \div 11 = 8$ remainder 2. Further, if $t = $ the apples left over, then $t = 2$.

➢ In other words, if we choose $x = 10$ and $k = 11$, the grocer has 8 customers and $t = 2$.

• To finish the problem, we simply need to **plug $x = 10$, $k = 11$, and $t = 2$ into the answer choices to see which one equals 8**. (Remember, the question asks for the number of customers). Doing so proves that (A) is the correct answer, since (A) is the only choice that equals 8:

$$\text{(A) } \frac{9x-t}{k} \quad \longrightarrow \quad \frac{9(10)-2}{11} = \frac{88}{11} = \boxed{8}$$

• Alternatively, we can use the "Hybrid strategy" discussed in our book on Arithmetic & "Plan B" Strategies to retrace the origin of our 8, like so:

$$8 = \frac{88}{11} = \frac{9(10)-2}{11} \longrightarrow \frac{9x-t}{k} = (A)$$

Rare or Advanced Concepts

(11) Linear Growth – Any problem in which something grows (or shrinks) in regular, identical increments is commonly known as a Linear Growth problem.

• Imagine a tree that grows 5 inches each year. That growth would be considered linear, since it occurs in identical increments (5 inches) and at regular intervals (each year).

➤ The easiest way to start a Linear Growth problem is with a T-CHART.

• In the left column, place the INTERVALS at which the growth occurs. In the right column, place any SIZES you know.

	MONTH	SIZE	
The growth happens	Now	42	The only sizes we
each month, so the	1		know are those NOW
INTERVALS are monthly.	2	48	and in 2 MONTHS
	3		

• For example, suppose that a certain bill increases x dollars each month, and that two months from now a bill that is currently $42 will be $48. You could represent that information as shown above.

➤ Then LABEL the unknown growth x. For every interval you "jump" down the t-chart, ADD an x to the size column.

MONTH	SIZE	
Now	42	
1	$42 + x$	x for ONE "jump"
2	48	from now. $3x$ for
3	$42 + 3x$	THREE "jumps" from now.

• As the chart shows, 2 months from now the bill is $48. However, 2 months from now the bill should ALSO be $42 + 2x$, since 2 months is TWO "jumps" down the t-chart. Thus, we know that $48 = $42 + 2x$.

• We can use this equation to determine that $x = 3. Since $x =$ the growth rate, we now know that each month raises the bill $3. As such, if we need to determine the size of the bill 10 months from now, we can add 10 "jumps" of $3 to the original bill of $42 to get $72.

- To get a better feel for Linear Growth, consider the following:

When a certain plant was first planted, it was 12 inches tall, and the height of the plant increased by a constant amount each day for the next 8 days. At the end of the 8th day, the plant was 20 percent taller than it was at the end of the 4th day.

Quantity A	**Quantity B**
The number of inches by which the height of the plant increased each day	0.8

- The problem states that the height of the plant increased by a **constant** amount **each** day. Because the plant's growth was linear, we can set up the following t-chart:

The growth happens each day, so the INTERVALS are daily.

DAY	SIZE	
Start	12	
1	$12 + x$	$4x$ for FOUR "jumps" from the start. $8x$ for
4	$12 + 4x$	EIGHT "jumps" from
8	$12 + 8x$	the start.

  ➢ As the chart shows, the plant's height was therefore $12 + 4x$ at the end of the 4th day and $12 + 8x$ at the end of the 8th day.

- The problem also states that the height of the plant was 20% taller at the end of the 8th day than it was at the end of the 4th day.

- Since the 8th day = $12 + 8x$ and the 4th day = $12 + 4x$, we can say:

"The **8th day** was **20% taller** than the **4th day.**"

$$12 + 8x = 1.2(12 + 4x)$$

  ➢ Solving the equation proves that $x = 0.75$, since:

$$12 + 8x = 14.4 + 4.8x \rightarrow 3.2x = 2.4 \rightarrow x = \frac{2.4}{3.2} = \frac{24}{32} = \frac{3}{4} = 0.75$$

- Because x = the number of inches by which the height of the plant increased each day, the correct answer is therefore (B).

(12) Integer Constraints – As you may recall from our book on <u>Number Properties &</u> <u>Algebra</u>, it is usually impossible to solve a single equation with two variables.

- That is, unless the problem requires the variables to be INTEGERS. In such cases, it is SOMETIMES possible to solve for both variables.

> ➤ To do so, you need to know something called the ADDITION or SUBTRACTION MULTIPLE RULE.

- In short, this rule states: **if two terms in an equation are multiples of** M**, then the remaining term in that equation must also be a multiple of** M.

- Take the equation $49 - x = 14$. Since 49 and 14 are both multiples of 7, x must also be a multiple of 7. Likewise, if $x + 18 = 42$, x must be a multiple of 2, 3, and 6, since 18 and 42 are both multiples of 2, 3, and 6.

> ➤ On rare occasions, this rule comes in handy with Quantity Mixture problems. To understand how, consider the following:

Zeke bought only apples and bananas. The apples cost $0.70 each and the bananas cost $0.90 each. If he bought $7.20 worth of fruit, how many apples and bananas did Zeke buy?

(A) 8 (B) 9 (C) 10 (D) 11 (E) 12

- According to the problem, apples cost $0.70, bananas cost $0.90, and Zeke spends $7.20 buying fruit. Thus, we know that $0.70a + 0.90b = 7.20$. If we multiply this equation by 10, we get:

$$7a + 9b = 72$$

> ➤ Since **apples and bananas cannot represent fractions**, this equation has an integer constraint: its variables must be integers.

- To solve for a and b, notice that $9b$ and 72 are both multiples of 9. This means that **7a must also be a multiple of 9**, such as 9, 18, or 27. If a were to equal 9, b would equal 1. But if a were to equal a larger multiple of 9, such as 18, b **would be negative**:

$$7(9) + 9b = 72 \qquad\qquad 7(18) + 9b = 72$$
$$9b = 9 \qquad\qquad\qquad 9b = -54$$
$$b = 1 \qquad\qquad\qquad b = -6$$

- Thus, when $a = 9$, $b = 1$, but when $a = 18$ or larger, b is negative. As such, a can only equal 9, meaning that b must equal 1. The correct answer is therefore (C), since $9 + 1 = 10$.

➤ Unfortunately, Algebraic Word Problems can involve integer constraints in other ways, too.

• In particular, watch out for questions asking "Which of the following COULD…" Such questions often imply a constraint on the possible quantities. Consider the following:

In 6 years, John will be 3 times as old as Fred. Which of the following could be John's current age?

A 35   B 36   C 37   D 38   E 39   F 40

• According to the problem, John will be three times as old as Fred in 6 years. Since both people have to age, we can translate this as:

"In 6 years, John will be 3 times as old as Fred."

$$j + 6 = 3(f + 6)$$

• Thus, $j + 6 = 3f + 18$.

➤ If we subtract 6 from both sides, we get $j = 3f + 12$. Therefore, John's current age MUST be 12 years greater than THREE TIMES Frank's current age.

• Since people's ages are given as whole numbers, not fractions, we know that John's age must be an integer.

• However, we also know that John's age must equal some MULTIPLE of 3.

➤ This goes back to the Addition and Subtraction Multiple Rule: if two terms in an equation are multiples of M, the remaining term must also be a multiple of M.

• Thus, if $j = 3f + 12$, then John's age must be a multiple of 3, since $3f$ and 12 are both multiples of 3.

• Since 36 and 39 are the only answers that are multiples of 3, John's age can only equal B and E.

> ➤ "Which of the following COULD ..." questions can be especially tricky if they involve FRACTIONAL relationships.

• With such problems, it's often useful to PICK NUMBERS to expose hidden constraints. Consider the following:

A certain classroom has $\frac{1}{5}$ fewer girls than boys. Which of the following could equal the total number of students in the class?

(A) 25   (B) 26   (C) 27   (D) 28   (E) 29

Answer: C. According to the problem, the classroom has $\frac{1}{5}$ fewer girls than boys. If we let the number of **boys = 10**, then the number of **girls = 8**, since $\frac{1}{5}$ of 10 = 2.

These numbers tell us that the ratio of boys to girls in the class must be 5 : 4, since $\frac{10}{8} = \frac{5}{4}$. If we insert the unknown multiplier into this ratio, we get **boys = 5x** and **girls = 4x**. Thus, the class has a **total of 9x students**, since $5x + 4x = 9x$.

If the total number of students equals $9x$, we know that our answer must be a MULTIPLE of 9: after all, any value for x that isn't an integer implies that the class has fractional boys or girls. The correct answer is therefore (C), since 27 is the only answer that is a multiple of 9.

> ➤ Here's a second example to help you get the hang of it:

In a recent poll, 1/3 more respondents answered "yes" than "no" to a certain question. If "yes" or "no" were the only responses, then the number of respondents could have equaled which of the following?

Indicate <u>all</u> such numbers.

A 63   B 65   C 67   D 68   E 69   F 70

Answer: A, F. According to the problem, the number of people who answered "yes" was $\frac{1}{3}$ greater than the number who answered "no". If we let the number of people who answered **"no" = 3**, then the number of people who answered **"yes" = 4**, since $\frac{1}{3}$ of 3 = 1.

These numbers tell us that the ratio of "yes" to "no" replies was 4 : 3. If we insert the unknown multiplier into this ratio, we get **"yes" respondents = 4x** and **"no" respondents = 3x**. Thus, there was a **total of 7x respondents**, since $4x + 3x = 7x$.

If the total number of respondents equals $7x$, our answer must be a MULTIPLE of 7. The correct answers are therefore (A) and (F), since 63 and 70 are both multiples of 7.

Drills

(13) Translation Drills – Translate each of the following statements.

Fundamental

1. 2 more than some number is 11.

2. Jack has a third of what Kevin has.

3. The product of two integers is 15.

4. 15 is 30 percent of what number?

5. x is 5 less than y.

6. What percent of 35 is 14?

7. The number of girls is 1 more than twice the number of boys.

8. Cara bought three apples and two bananas for five dollars.

Intermediate

9. What is 30 percent of 40 percent of w?

10. Two less than a certain number is more than half that number.

11. A certain class has twice as many girls as boys.

12. Five years ago, Alex was twice as as old as Bill.

13. Maia earns 1/3 less than Sarah.

14. x yards of silk at y dollars a yard cost 8 dollars.

Tricky

15. At most, Brenda earns 1/4 more than Callie.

16. Eight is equal to how many halves of eight?

17. John's monthly salary is equal to 8 percent of his sales in excess of $1,000.

18. If 3 cups of water are added to a jar that is half full of water, the water in the jar will increase by 1/3.

Solutions

1. A translation is simply an algebra equation written with words instead of math symbols.

2 **more than** some number **is** 11.

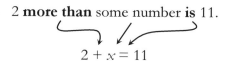

$2 + x = 11$

2. Always translate the words in the ORDER that the information is given. The sequence of your equation should match the sequence of the words.

Jack **has** a third **of** what Kevin has.

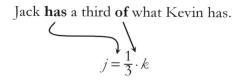

$j = \frac{1}{3} \cdot k$

3. Most "translation words" are obvious. In some cases, however, they may not be. If you have yet to do so, be sure to go through our lists in sections two and five.

The **product** of **two integers** is 15.

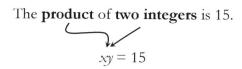

$xy = 15$

4. The word PERCENT means "divided by 100", so percent relationships can often be solved as translations:

15 **is** 30 **percent** of **what number?**

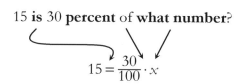

$15 = \frac{30}{100} \cdot x$

5. If one term is "some amount" less than another, that amount must be SUBTRACTED from the SECOND term:

x **is** 5 **less than** y.

$x = y - 5$

6. WHAT PERCENT can be translated as "x divided by 100":

What percent **of** 35 **is** 14?

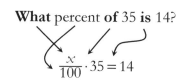

$\frac{x}{100} \cdot 35 = 14$

7. Whenever possible, use MEANINGFUL variables in place of x and y.

The number of girls **is 1 more than** twice the number of boys.

$$g = 1 + 2b$$

8. The Quantity Mixture formula: $\text{Rate}_1 \times \text{Quantity}_1 + \text{Rate}_2 \times \text{Quantity}_2 = \text{Total Cost}$

Cara bought **3 apples** and **2 bananas** for **5 dollars**.

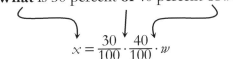

$$3a + 2b = 5$$

9. When translating, let the words do the work. Always follow the order of the words:

What is 30 percent **of** 40 percent **of** w?

$$x = \frac{30}{100} \cdot \frac{40}{100} \cdot w$$

10. LESS THAN "some amount" means "subtraction". LESS THAN means "inequality":

Two less than a certain number **is more than** half that number.

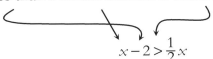

$$x - 2 > \frac{1}{2}x$$

11. To translate "AS MANY AS", always multiply the term after the SECOND AS.

A certain class has **twice** as many girls **as** boys.

$$g = 2b$$

12. For age problems, remember that BOTH people must age:

Five years ago, Alex **was** twice as old **as** Bill.

$$a - 5 = 2(b - 5)$$

13. Phrases such as LESS THAN and GREATER THAN are tricky when used with FRACTIONS. Be sure to add or subtract the fraction from the original amount:

Maia **earns** 1/3 **less than** Sarah.

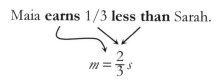

$$m = \frac{2}{3}s$$

14. AT means "multiply":

x yards of silk **at** y dollars a yard **cost** 8 dollars.

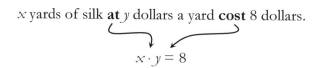

$$x \cdot y = 8$$

15. AT MOST means "less than or equal to":

At most, Brenda **earns** 1/4 **more than** Callie.

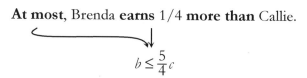

$$b \le \frac{5}{4}c$$

16. No matter how simple something seems, don't overthink it. Let the words do the work.

Eight is **equal** to **how many** halves **of** eight?

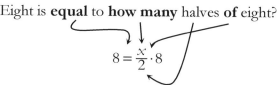

$$8 = \frac{x}{2} \cdot 8$$

17. IN EXCESS OF means "subtract":

John's monthly salary **is equal** to 8 percent **of** his sales **in excess of** $1,000.

$$j = \frac{8}{100} \times (s - 1,000)$$

18. INCREASE BY "1/3" does NOT mean "multiply by 1/3", since multiplying something by 1/3 actually decreases it. Such a phrase means "multiply by 1/3 more than the original amount", which is 4/3:

If 3 cups of water are **added** to a **jar that is half full** of water, **the water in the jar** will **increase by 1/3**.

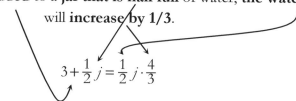

$$3 + \frac{1}{2}j = \frac{1}{2}j \cdot \frac{4}{3}$$

Practice Questions

(14) Problem Sets – The following questions have been arranged into three groups: fundamental, intermediate, and rare or advanced.

• Whether you're aiming for a perfect score or a score closer to average, mastery of the concepts in the FUNDAMENTAL questions is absolutely essential.

➢ As you might expect, the INTERMEDIATE questions are more difficult but are essential for test-takers who need an above-average score or higher.

• Finally, the RARE or ADVANCED questions test concepts that are very sophisticated or seldom encountered on the GRE. Mastery of such questions is required only if you need a math score above the 90th percentile.

• As always, if you find yourself confused, bogged down with busy work, or stuck, don't be afraid to fall back on your "Plan B" strategies!

Fundamental

1. If $\frac{1}{6}$ of a certain number is 4, then $\frac{1}{8}$ of the number is

   (A) $\frac{4}{7}$ (B) $\frac{3}{2}$ (C) $\frac{7}{4}$ (D) 3   (E) 24

> 8 is n percent of 40.
> p is 25 percent of 105.

	Quantity A	Quantity B
2.	n	p

3. If one number exceeds another number by 12 and the larger number is 4/3 times the smaller number, then the smaller number is

   (A) 12   (B) 36   (C) 42   (D) 48   (E) 64

4. The total amount of Michaela's water bill for the last month was $38.50. The bill consisted of a fixed charge of $13.50 plus a charge of $0.05 for each gallon used. For how many gallons was Michaela charged?

Quantity A	Quantity B

5. The cost of p pears at a cost of $k + 5$ cents apiece | The cost of k kiwis at a cost of $p + 5$ cents apiece

6. If n is positive and p is 9 less than the square of n, which of the following expresses n in terms of p?

(A) $n = p^2 - 9$ (B) $n = p^2 + 3$ (C) $n = \sqrt{p} + 3$
(D) $n = \sqrt{9 - p}$ (E) $n = \sqrt{p + 9}$

Quantity A	Quantity B

7. 35 percent of $\frac{5}{7}$ of 60 | $\frac{7}{9}$ percent of $\frac{3}{14}$ of 1,800

get rid of decimals

8. Kayla has 32 stamps, some worth $0.35 and some worth $0.40. If the combined value of the stamps is $12.40, how many $0.35 stamps does Kayla have?

9. John recently purchased a jacket and a shirt. The cost of the shirt was $42 less than the cost of the jacket. If the cost of the jacket was 5/3 the cost of the shirt, how much did the shirt cost?

(A) $45 (B) $50 (C) $54 (D) $63 (E) $90

10. Five is equal to how many thirds of five?

(A) $\frac{1}{5}$ (B) $\frac{1}{3}$ (C) 3 (D) 5 (E) 15

11. Jan's weekly salary is n dollars. Each week, she uses $\frac{4n}{5}$ dollars for expenses and saves the rest. At those rates, how many weeks will it take Jan to save $500, in terms of n?

   (A) $\frac{500}{n}$ (B) $\frac{2,500}{n}$ (C) $\frac{n}{625}$ (D) $\frac{n}{2,500}$ (E) $625n$

15 percent of 10 percent of a certain number equals 75 percent of r percent of that same number.

Quantity A	Quantity B
r	2

12.

Intermediate

---

7 years ago, Fred was half as old as Hank.
Hank is now 15 years older than Fred.

Quantity A	Quantity B
Hank's age 6 years from now	Twice Fred's current age

13.

In a group of 40 employees, the number of managers was 4 more than three times the number of production workers, and 3/5 of the employees were neither managers nor production workers.

Quantity A	Quantity B
The number of production workers in the group	5

14.

15. Jane received 2/5 of her aunt's estate, and each of her two sisters received 1/2 of the balance. If Jane and one of her sisters received a total of $56,000 from the estate, what was the amount of the estate?

   (A) 72,000   (B) 80,000   (C) 84,000   (D) 90,000   (E) 96,000

16. If x years ago Chelsea's age was 8, and x years from now it will be $3x$, how old will Chelsea be in $5x$ years?

   (A) 15   (B) 23   (C) 24   (D) 40   (E) 56

A carton of erasers can be purchased for $4.00, or n erasers can be purchased at a cost of $0.19 per eraser.

	Quantity A	Quantity B
17.	The greatest possible value of n if the cost of purchasing the n erasers is less than the cost of purchasing the carton	21

18. Two years ago, Maxine spent between 1/3 and 2/5 of her gross income on rental payments for her apartment. If Maxine spent $16,120 on rental payments two years ago, which of the following could have been her gross income two years ago?

Indicate <u>all</u> such gross incomes.

A $40,030   B $43,180   C $44,280   D $48,306   E $50,260

19. Jim's compensation for any week is $420 plus 4 percent of his total sales in excess of $1,200 for that week. Wendy's compensation for any week is 6 percent of her total sales for that week. For what amount of total weekly sales would Jim and Wendy earn the same compensation?

20. If an integer n is subtracted from an integer p and the result is less than p, then n is

(A) equal to p (B) less than 0   (C) less than p
(D) greater than 0   (E) greater than p

21. Today is Amanda's 8th birthday and her mother's 36th birthday. How many years from today will Amanda's mother be three times as old as Amanda is at that time?

(A) 4   (B) 5   (C) 6   (D) 7   (E) 8

22. If a is 30 percent of b and 25 percent of b is 30, then 9 is what percent of a?

(A) 12.5   (B) 25   (C) 40   (D) 60   (E) 75

Jar A contains k more than twice the marbles in jar B, and the two jars together contain a total of 60 marbles.

Quantity A	Quantity B
23. Three times the number of marbles contained in jar B	$60 - k$

To reproduce an photograph, a shop charges d dollars to make a negative, $\frac{2d}{5}$ dollars for each of the first 15 prints, and $\frac{d}{5}$ dollars for each print in excess of 15 prints. The total charge to make a negative and 30 prints from an old photograph is $70.

Quantity A	Quantity B
24. d	7.5

25. If a certain state's rainfall in May was 1/4 of its rainfall in June, and its rainfall in July was 3/5 of its rainfall in May, then the state's rainfall in June was how many times the average of its rainfalls in May and July?

$$(A)\ 2 \quad (B)\ 3 \quad (C)\ 4 \quad (D)\ 5 \quad (E)\ 6$$

26. The cost, in dollars, of manufacturing w washing machines is $7{,}000 + 300w$. The amount received when selling these washing machines is $400w$ dollars. Which of the following represents a possible number of washing machines that can be manufactured and sold so that the amount received is at least equal to the manufacturing cost?

Select all possible numbers.

$\boxed{A}$ 60 $\quad$ $\boxed{B}$ 65 $\quad$ $\boxed{C}$ 70 $\quad$ $\boxed{D}$ 75 $\quad$ $\boxed{E}$ 80

27. A certain jar is 2/5 full of water. A second jar, which has twice the capacity of the first, is 1/4 full of water. If all of the water in the second jar were to be poured into the first, then the first jar would be filled to what fraction of its capacity?

$$(A)\ \frac{9}{20} \quad (B)\ \frac{3}{5} \quad (C)\ \frac{4}{5} \quad (D)\ \frac{7}{8} \quad (E)\ \frac{9}{10}$$

28. On a test, one point is given for every correct answer and one-fifth of a point is taken away for every blank or incorrect answer. Serena answered all 80 questions on the test and received a score of 56, how many questions did she answer correctly?

(A) 50   (B) 55   (C) 60   (D) 65   (E) 70

In a certain class, there are 3 times as many boys as girls. If 3 girls were to leave and 4 boys to be added, there would be 4 times as many boys as girls.

	Quantity A	Quantity B
29.	The number of boys and girls currently in the class	75

30. At 10 years old, Colleen was 4 feet tall. Her height increased by some constant amount each year for the next 8 years. At 16, she was 1/5 taller than she was at 13. How much did she grow each year, in feet?

(A) $\frac{1}{6}$ (B) $\frac{1}{5}$ (C) $\frac{1}{4}$ (D) $\frac{1}{3}$ (E) $\frac{1}{2}$

Lynn has $8n$ red marbles and $6k$ blue marbles. John has half as many red marbles as Lynn, but he has twice as many red marbles and blue marbles combined as Lynn.

	Quantity A	Quantity B
31.	The number of blue marbles that John has	$12n + 12k$

32. Lee bought only $0.70 stamps and $0.40 stamps. If he bought $6.30 worth of stamps, which of the following could equal the number of $0.70 stamps that Lee bought?

Select all possible numbers.

A 1   B 4   C 5   D 7   E 14

33. Positive integer a is 25 percent of 25 percent of positive integer b, and a percent of b equals 16. What is the value of b?

(A) 80   (B) 120   (C) 160   (D) 200   (E) 240

34. If p percent of q is decreased by p percent, what is the result in terms of p and q?

(A) $\dfrac{pq(100-p)}{10,000}$ (B) $\dfrac{1}{pq(100-p)}$ (C) $\dfrac{pq}{100}$ (D) $\dfrac{1,000\,p}{pq(100-p)}$ (E) $\dfrac{pq(100+p)}{100}$

35. The total amount that Hilary paid for a meal was equal to the price of the meal plus a sales tax that was 8 percent of the price of the meal. Hilary paid for the meal with a $20 bill and received the correct change, which was less than $2.00. Which of the following statements must be true?

Indicate <u>all</u> such statements.

A The price of the meal was less than $18.50.

B The price of the meal was greater than $16.75.

C The sales tax was less than $0.85.

(15) Solutions – Video solutions for each of the previous questions can be found on our website at **www.sherpaprep.com/videos**.

• BOOKMARK this address for future visits!

> ➤ To view the videos, you'll need the LOGIN and PASSWORD that you created upon registering your copy of Word Problems.

• If you have yet to register your book yet, please go to **www.sherpaprep.com/activate** and enter your email address, last name, and shipping address.

• Be sure to provide the SAME last name and shipping address that you used to purchase your copy of Master Key to the GRE or to enroll in your GRE course with Sherpa Prep!

> ➤ When checking your answers, we encourage you to watch the solution for any problem that you answered INCORRECTLY

• The same goes for any problem that took you MORE than TWO MINUTES to solve.

• After digesting the explanation, REVISIT your mistake a couple of days later to ensure that the problem no longer poses issues to you.

> ➤ If you struggle to solve the problem a SECOND time, add it to your "LOG of ERRORS" and redo it every few weeks.

• Solving tricky questions MORE THAN ONCE is the best way to learn from your mistakes and to avoid similar difficulties on your actual exam.

Fundamental		Intermediate		Rare or Advanced	
1. D	11. B	13. B	23. C	28. C	
2. B	12. C	14. B	24. B	29. B	
3. B		15. B	25. D	30. D	
4. 500		16. E	26. C, D, E	31. C	
5. D		17. C	27. E	32. A, C	
6. E		18. B, C, D		33. C	
7. A		19. 18,600		34. A	
8. 8		20. D		35. B	
9. D		21. C			
10. C		22. B			

Chapter 4

Ratios & Proportions

Ratios & Proportions

To be discussed:

Fundamental Concepts

Whether you're aiming for a perfect score or a score closer to average, mastery of the following concepts is essential.

Rare or Advanced Concepts

The following concepts are either advanced or are tested only on rare occasions. If you don't need an elite math score, don't waste your time!

Practice Questions

There's no substitute for elbow grease. Practice your new skills to ensure that you internalize what you've studied.

Fundamental Concepts

---

(1) Introduction – A ratio is a direct relationship in which two or more quantities increase, or decrease, by the SAME factor.

• If one item in that relationship goes up by a factor of 3, so do the others. If one item in that relationship goes down by a factor of 5, so do the others.

> In math, there are three ways to express a ratio, all of which you may encounter on the GRE:

1. With the words "to" or "for every".
2. As a fraction.
3. With a colon.

• For example, if a bowl contains 2 red apples for every 3 green apples, the relationship between the number of red apples and the number of green apples can be expressed as:

$$2 \text{ red apples to } 3 \text{ green apples} \qquad \frac{2 \text{ red apples}}{3 \text{ green apples}} \qquad 2 \text{ red apples} : 3 \text{ green apples}$$

> When expressing relationships as ratios, be sure to **express the elements in the order that they are given**.

• For example, if a grocer sells 5 apples for every 2 pears, that ratio would properly be expressed as $5 : 2$ or $\frac{5}{2}$.

• If the ratio were represented as $2 : 5$ or $\frac{2}{5}$, the expression would erroneously indicate that five pears were sold for every 2 apples.

> Finally, it's important to remember that **ratios express RELATIVE relationships**, not exact quantities.

• In most cases, ratios do not provide enough information to determine the exact number of elements being compared.

• For example, if a jar contains 3 green marbles for every 5 yellow marbles, we do not know how many green and yellow marbles the jar actually holds. That jar could contain 3 green marbles and 5 yellow marbles, or 6 green marbles and 10 yellow marbles, or any other combinations of numbers whose ratio is 3 to 5.

(2) Simplifying Ratios – There are a variety of ways to simplify ratios.

➤ In most instances, the best way to simplify a ratio is to EXPRESS the terms as a FRACTION.

• Once a ratio is expressed in fraction form, its terms can be reduced with the same techniques that are used to simplify all fractions.

• Consider the following:

The ratio of $\frac{14}{9}$ to $\frac{21}{12}$ is equal to

(A) 4 to 9   (B) 2 to 3   (C) 8 to 9   (D) 7 to 6   (E) 4 to 3

Answer: C. Expressing $\frac{14}{9}$ to $\frac{21}{12}$ as a fraction gives us $\dfrac{\frac{14}{9}}{\frac{21}{12}}$.

Like any "fraction containing fractions", we can simplify this fraction by multiplying the numerator by the "flip" of its denominator. Doing so proves that (C) is the correct answer, as:

$$\frac{\frac{14}{9}}{\frac{21}{12}} = \frac{14}{9} \times \frac{12}{21} = \frac{2(\cancel{7})}{3(\cancel{3})} \times \frac{\cancel{4}(4)}{3(\cancel{7})} = \frac{2}{3} \cdot \frac{4}{3} = \frac{8}{9}$$

➤ In RARE instances, a ratio may contain 3 or more terms. You can simplify such ratios by FACTORING the terms.

• Consider the following:

Which of the following is equal to the ratio of 14 to 56 to 84?

(A) 1 : 3 : 8   (B) 1 : 4 : 6   (C) 2 : 5 : 7   (D) 2 : 6 : 9   (E) 2 : 7 : 12

Answer: B. To simplify the ratio 14 : 56 : 84, we can factor out a 7. Doing so shows us that the ratio simplifies to 2 : 8 : 12, as:

$$14 : 56 : 84 = \cancel{7}(2) : \cancel{7}(8) : \cancel{7}(12)$$

However, since we can further simplify 2 : 8 : 12 by factoring out a 2, the ratio 14 : 56 : 84 fully simplifies to 1 : 4 : 6, as:

$$2 : 8 : 12 = \cancel{2}(1) : \cancel{2}(4) : \cancel{2}(6)$$

> ➤ In RARE instances, a ratio with 3 or more terms may sometimes contain fractions.

• To simplify such monstrosities, multiply the ratio by the LEAST COMMON DENOMINATOR of the fractions.

• Consider the following:

The ratio of $\frac{5}{6}$ to $\frac{2}{3}$ to $\frac{1}{2}$ is equal to

(A) $5:2:1$ (B) $5:4:2$ (C) $5:4:3$ (D) $5:4:6$ (E) $5:12:18$

Answer. C. To simplify the ratio $\frac{5}{6}:\frac{2}{3}:\frac{1}{2}$, we need to multiply it by the least common denominator of the fractions, which is 6. Doing so proves that (C) is the answer, since:

$$6\left(\frac{5}{6}:\frac{2}{3}:\frac{1}{2}\right) = 6\times\frac{5}{6}:6\times\frac{2}{3}:6\times\frac{1}{2} = 5:4:3$$

> ➤ Finally, in RARE instances, a ratio with 3 or more terms may occasionally contain decimals.

• To simplify such ratios, MULTIPLY the ratio by a POWER of TEN to rid the ratio of decimals.

• Consider the following:

Which of the following is equal to the ratio of 3 to 0.09 to 0.6?

(A) $15:4:8$ (B) $25:4:12$ (C) $30:5:12$ (D) $60:5:24$ (E) $100:3:20$

Answer. E. To simplify the ratio of 3 to 0.09 to 0.6, we first need to multiply it by 100 to remove its decimals. Doing so gives us:

$$100(3:0.09:0.6) = 300:9:60$$

Then we need to reduce the ratio by factoring it. Since 300, 9, and 60 share a common factor of 3, the correct answer must be (E):

$$300:9:60 = 3(100):3(3):3(20) = 100:3:20$$

(3) Algebraic Ratios – From time to time, GRE problems require the conversion of equations such as $3x = 4y$ or $2y = 7x$ into ratios, typically as a step to a more complex goal.

• For example, given the statement $3x = 4y$, you may need to determine the ratio of x to y or the ratio of y to x.

➢ There are many ways to do so. If you already have a method: great. Feel free to stick with it.

• If you don't, first ISOLATE one of the variables. For example, if $2a = 7b$, and you need to determine the ratio of a to b, first isolate a as follows:

$$2a = 7b \;\rightarrow\; a = \frac{7b}{2}$$

• Then DIVIDE both sides of the equation by the OTHER variable. Thus, the ratio of a to b is 7 to 2, since:

$$a = \frac{7b}{2} \;\rightarrow\; \frac{a}{b} = \frac{7b}{2b} \;\rightarrow\; \frac{a}{b} = \frac{7}{2}$$

Divide BOTH sides by b

➢ Note that if we need to determine the ratio of b to a (instead of a to b), we can simply FLIP the ratio of a to b.

• In other words, if the ratio of a to b is 7 to 2, then the ratio of b to a is 2 to 7, since:

$$\frac{a}{b} = \frac{7}{2} \;\rightarrow\; \frac{b}{a} = \frac{2}{7} \quad \text{(flip both sides!)}$$

• To get a better feel for converting algebraic equations into ratios, let's work through a sample problem together:

If $4r = 6s$, then the ratio of s to r is

(A) 2 to 3   (B) 2 to 5   (C) 3 to 5   (D) 3 to 2   (E) 5 to 2

Answer. A. To determine the ratio of s to r, first isolate r and then divide both sides of the equation by s, the OTHER variable:

$$4r = 6s \;\rightarrow\; r = \frac{6s}{4} \;\rightarrow\; \frac{r}{s} = \frac{6s}{4s} \;\rightarrow\; \frac{r}{s} = \frac{3}{2}$$

Then FLIP the ratio of r to s. Since the ratio of r to s is $\frac{3}{2}$, the ratio of s to r is thus $\frac{2}{3}$.

(4) "Part-to-Whole" vs. "Part-to-Part" Ratios – All ratios can be described as either "part-to-whole" ratios or "part-to-part" ratios.

"Part-to-Whole"	**"Part-to-Part"**
"Part-to-Whole" ratios express the relationship between an **entire group** and **part** of that group.	"Part-to-part" ratios express the relationship between **groups that do not overlap**.

• For instance, a class that has 5 boys for every 8 students is a "part-to-whole" ratio, since the number of boys in the class is a **subset** of the total number of students.

• Conversely, a class that has 5 boys for every 3 girls is a "part-to-part" ratio, since there is no overlap between the number of boys in the class and the number of girls. Each group represents an **independent segment** of the entire class.

➢ When working with ratios, it can sometimes be helpful to convert "part-to-whole" ratios into "part-to-part" ratios, or vice versa.

• To do so, simply remember that the **SUM of the PARTS equals the WHOLE**. For example, if a class has 4 boys for every 9 children, then that class has 4 boys for every 5 girls, since 4 boys + 5 girls = 9 children.

• Likewise, if a class has 3 boys for every 5 girls, then that class has 3 boys for every 8 children (or 5 girls for every 8 children), since 3 boys + 5 girls = 8 children.

➢ To get a sense of how this might help you solve a GRE ratio problem, consider the following:

A solution contains only water and iodine. If the ratio of ounces of solution to ounces of water is 7 : 5, what is the ratio of ounces of iodine to ounces of water in the solution?

(A) $\frac{1}{6}$ (C) $\frac{2}{7}$ (C) $\frac{2}{5}$ (D) $\frac{5}{12}$ (E) $\frac{7}{12}$

Answer: C. If the solution consists of 7 parts, and 5 of those parts are water, then 2 of those parts must be iodine, since **water + iodine = solution**. Thus, the ratio of iodine to water is 2 : 5, as the solution consists of 2 parts iodine and 5 parts water.

(5) The Unknown Multiplier – As we've seen, ratios don't always tell us the EXACT quantities within a relationship.

• For example, if a jar contains 4 blue marbles for every 5 red marbles, we do not know how many blue and red marbles the jar contains.

➢ The jar may contain 4 blue marbles and 5 red marbles, or any one of an infinite number of combinations whose ratio is 4 to 5, such as:

<table>
<tr><td>8 blue marbles</td><td>10 red marbles</td></tr>
<tr><td>12 blue marbles</td><td>15 red marbles</td></tr>
<tr><td>16 blue marbles</td><td>20 red marbles</td></tr>
</table>

• When ratios do not indicate exact quantities, the relationships that they express are only RELATIVE.

➢ Algebraically, relative relationships can be expressed by means of a variable x that is commonly referred to as the UNKNOWN MULTIPLIER.

• For example, a ratio of 4 blue marbles for every 5 red marbles could be expressed as $4:5$, but a setup of $4x:5x$ more accurately represents the relationship, since we don't know the exact number of blue or red marbles.

• In other words, a relationship such as 4 blue marbles for every 5 red marbles is MOST ACCURATELY expressed as:

$$\frac{4 \text{ blue marbles}}{5 \text{ red marbles}} = \frac{4x}{5x}$$

➢ Using the unknown multiplier is the KEY to solving more difficult ratio problems. Labeling EACH part of a ratio with an x will help you to identify EXACT values.

• Imagine that the angles of a triangle are in the ratio $2:3:4$ and that you need to determine the measure of the largest angle. The angles of a triangle add to 180°, so the largest angle can't have a measure of 4°, since 2° + 3° + 4° don't add to 180°.

➢ However, if we use the unknown multiplier to represent the ratio of the angles as $2x:3x:4x$, we know that $2x + 3x + 4x = 180°$.

• From this, we also know that $x = 20°$, since $9x = 180°$.

• Thus, the unknown multiplier allows us to determine that the largest angle in this triangle has a measure of 80°, since the largest angle in the ratio equals $4x = 4(20°) = 80°$.

(6) "Part-to-Part" Ratios – When working with "PART-TO-PART" ratios, be sure to use the unknown multiplier.

• Such ratios are ALWAYS RELATIVE. They never indicate the exact quantities of their groups. Consider the following:

The ratio of boys to girls on a certain bus is 7 to 5. If there are 42 boys on the bus, and 3 girls then exit, how many girls remain?

(A) 21 (B) 24 (C) 25 (D) 27 (E) 28

Answer. D. The relationship between boys and girls is a "part-to-part" relationship, since boys and girls each represent independent segments of children on the bus.

➤ "Part-to-part" relationships are relative, so the ratio between them can be set up with the unknown multiplier. Doing so here gives us:

boys : girls

$7x : 5x$

• Since the number of boys can be represented as $7x$, and the problem states that there are 42 boys, $7x$ must equal 42. If $7x = 42$, then $x = 6$. Plugging the unknown multiplier back into the ratio shows that the bus started with 30 girls, since the number of girls = $5x$, and $5(6) = 30$. If 3 girls then leave, 27 remain on the bus.

The ratio of peanuts to almonds to hazelnuts in a bowl of nuts is 5 : 4 : 2. If there are 99 nuts in the bowl, and every nut is either a peanut, almond, or hazelnut, how many hazelnuts does the mix contain?

(A) 12 (B) 14 (C) 15 (D) 17 (E) 18

Answer. E. The relationship between peanuts, almonds, and walnuts is a "part-to-part" relationship, since each type of nut represents an independent segment of the mixture.

➤ "Part-to-part" relationships are relative, so the ratio between them can be set up with the unknown multiplier. Doing so here gives us:

peanuts : almonds : hazelnuts

$5x : 4x : 2x$

• Since the bowl only contains peanuts, almonds, and hazelnuts, $5x + 4x + 2x$ must equal 99. If $11x = 99$, then $x = 9$. Plugging the unknown multiplier back into the ratio shows that there are 18 hazelnuts, since the number of hazelnuts = $2x$, and $2(9) = 18$.

(7) "Part-to-Whole Ratios": Think Proportion! – Unlike "part-to-part" ratios, "part-to-whole" ratios almost always involve real values.

• As such, they rarely require the use of the unknown multiplier.

➤ Further, "part-to-whole" ratio problems almost never use the word "ratio". Thus, they can be DIFFICULT to spot.

• Unfortunately, there's no easy tip we can give you to help you identify problems involving "part-to-whole" ratios.

• It's worth pointing out, however, that such problems often involve a chemical solution and one of its ingredients, a group of people and a subset of that group, or a budget and a portion of that budget.

➤ Fortunately, however, "part-to-whole" ratio problems are EASY to solve.

• First set up a PROPORTION in which the part is compared to the whole. To ensure that you do so correctly, LABEL each UNIT within the proportion:

$$\frac{PART}{WHOLE} = \frac{PART}{WHOLE}$$

• Then cross-multiply to solve the proportion. To get a sense of how this works, consider the following:

An iodine solution contains 3.6 grams of iodine per 120 cubic centimeters of solution. If 72 cubic centimeters of the solution were poured into an empty beaker, approximately how many grams of iodine would the beaker hold?

(A) 1.4   (B) 1.6   (C) 1.8   (D) 2.0   (E) 2.2

Answer. E. Because iodine is **part of the solution**, the relationship between iodine and solution is a "part-to-whole" relationship. Therefore, the amount of iodine in the beaker can be determined with the following proportion:

$$\frac{part}{whole}: \quad \frac{3.6 \text{ iodine}}{120 \text{ solution}} = \frac{x \text{ iodine}}{72 \text{ solution}}$$

To avoid silly mistakes, always LABEL the items in a proportion!

Cross-multiplication shows that x = 2.2 grams of iodine, approximately, as:

$$72(3.6) = 120x \quad \Rightarrow \quad x = \frac{72(3.6)}{120} = \frac{6(12)(3.6)}{10(12)} = \frac{6(3.6)}{10} = \frac{21.6}{10} = 2.16 \text{ grams}$$

➢ To give you a better sense of what "part-to-whole" ratio problems look like, here are two more examples for you:

The annual budget of company K is to be shown on a circle graph. If the size of each sector of the graph is to be proportional to the amount of the budget that it represents, and $1.2 million represents a sector that comprises 54 degrees of the circle, what is the annual budget of company K, in millions of dollars?

(A) 7.8   (B) 8.0   (C) 8.1   (D) 8.2   (E) 8.4

Answer: B. Because a circle contains a total of 360 degrees, and a sector of 54 degrees comprises **part of that circle**, the relationship between the $1.2 million sector and the entire budget is a "part-to-whole" relationship. As such, the annual budget of company K can be determined with the following proportion:

$$\frac{part}{whole}: \quad \frac{54°}{360°} = \frac{1.2 \text{ million}}{x \text{ million}}$$

Cross-multiplication shows that $x = \$8$ million, as:

$$54x = 1.2(360) \quad \rightarrow \quad x = \frac{1.2(360)}{54} = \frac{1.2(10)(36)}{6(9)} = \frac{\cancel{12}(36)}{\cancel{6}(9)} = 2(4) = \$8 \text{ million}$$

36 starlings were recently introduced into forest F. Two months later, 108 birds from the forest were caught, of which 4 were found to have been starlings. If the percent of starlings caught approximates the percent of starlings in the forest, what is the approximate number of birds in forest F?

(A) 848   (B) 916   (C) 972   (D) 1,012   (E) 1,096

Answer: C. Because starlings comprise **part of the birds** in forest F, the relationship between starlings and birds is a "part-to-whole" relationship. Therefore, the number of birds in the forest can be determined with the following proportion:

$$\frac{part}{whole}: \quad \frac{4 \text{ starlings}}{108 \text{ birds}} = \frac{36 \text{ starlings}}{x \text{ birds}}$$

Cross-multiplication shows that $x = 972$ birds, approximately, as:

$$4x = 36(108) \quad \rightarrow \quad x = \frac{\cancel{36}(108)}{\cancel{4}} = 9(108) = 972 \text{ birds}$$

(8) Comparing Apples to Oranges? Think Proportion! – Proportions can also be used to solve problems comparing "apples-to-oranges".

• A relationship between two UNRELATED objects or measurements can be thought of as an "apples-to-oranges" relationship.

➤ The correlations of a wall to a shadow, a mile to a kilometer, or a group of birds to a group of trees are all examples of such relationships.

• If the relationship between the two objects is a DIRECT one, an INCREASE in one quantity will result in an INCREASE in the other.

• Likewise, a DECREASE in one quantity in a direct relationship will result in a DECREASE in the other.

➤ To solve problems involving direct correlations, simply set up an "apples-to-oranges" proportion, like this:

$$\frac{APPLES}{ORANGES} = \frac{APPLES}{ORANGES}$$

To avoid silly mistakes, be sure to LABEL the items in your proportions!

• Let's work through a sample problem together:

2.5 reams of brand B paper contain a total of 900 sheets.

Quantity A	**Quantity B**
The number of sheets in 1.5 reams of brand B paper	560

Answer: B. The correlation of reams to sheets is an "apples-to-oranges" correlation. Since 2.5 reams contain 900 sheets of paper, we can set up the following proportion:

$$\frac{apples}{oranges}: \quad \frac{2.5 \text{ reams}}{900 \text{ sheets}} = \frac{1.5 \text{ reams}}{x \text{ sheets}}$$

➤ If we cross-multiply this equation, we get $2.5x = 1.5(900)$. Dividing both sides by 2.5 then proves that $x = 540$, since:

$$x = \frac{1.5(900)}{2.5} = \frac{15(900)}{25} = \frac{15(100)(9)}{25} = 15(4)(9) = 60(9) = 540 \text{ sheets}$$

• Thus, the correct answer is (B).

➢ To be sure that you've got the hang of it, let's work through a second example together

- This one is a bit trickier:

A 36-inch yardstick is marked off in twelfths of an inch. In inches, what is the length, in inches, from the zero mark to the 102nd mark of the yardstick?

(A) 7.9   (B) 8.3   (C) 8.5   (D) 8.7   (E) 9.0

Answer: C. The correlation of marks to inches is an "apples-to-oranges" correlation. Since the yardstick contains 12 marks for every inch, we can set up the following proportion:

$$\frac{apples}{oranges}: \quad \frac{1 \text{ inch}}{12 \text{ marks}} = \frac{x \text{ inches}}{102 \text{ marks}}$$

➢ If we cross-multiply this equation, we get $12x = 102$. Dividing both sides by 12 then proves that $x = 8.5$, since:

$$x = \frac{102}{12} = \frac{51}{6} = \frac{3(17)}{3(2)} = 8.5 \text{ inches}$$

- Thus, the correct answer is (C).

(9) Inverse Proportions – Any relationship in which one quantity increases while another quantity decreases is known as an inverse proportion.

- For example, the relationship between time and speed would be considered inversely proportional, since the time it takes to travel a certain distance **decreases** as a traveler's speed **increases**.

  ➤ To solve an inverse proportion, simply SET the PRODUCTS of the two quantities EQUAL to one another.

- To get a proper sense of how to do this, consider the following:

If 8 workers, working non-stop at uniform rates, can assemble a certain machine in 6 hours, how many hours would it take 12 workers, working non-stop at identical uniform rates, to assemble the same machine?

(A) 3   (B) 3.6   (C) 4   (D) 4.2   (E) 4.8

Answer: C. Because the amount of time needed to assemble the machine should **decrease** as the number of workers **increases**, this is an inverse proportion. To solve it, we need to set the **product** of 8 workers × 6 hours equal to the **product** of 12 workers × h hours:

$$8 \text{ workers} \times 6 \text{ hours} = 12 \text{ workers} \times h \text{ hours}$$
$$8(6) = 12(h)$$
$$h = 48/12 = 4$$

Thus, it would take 12 workers 4 hours to assemble the same machine.

Tank T has enough water to supply 20 people for 24 days. At the same average rate of consumption, how many days can the tank supply 16 people?

(A) 18   (B) 21   (C) 27   (D) 30   (E) 33

Answer: D. Because the number of days that the tank can supply water should **increase** as the number of people it supplies **decreases**, this is an inverse proportion. To solve it, we need to set the **product** of 20 people × 24 days equal to the **product** of 16 people × d days:

$$16 \text{ people} \times d \text{ days} = 20 \text{ people} \times 24 \text{ days}$$
$$16d = 20(24)$$
$$d = \frac{20(24)}{16} = \frac{\cancel{20}(24)}{\cancel{16}(4)} = 5(6) = 30 \text{ days}$$

Thus, the tank can supply 16 people with water for 30 days.

Rare or Advanced Concepts
---

(10) Independent Ratios, Different Multipliers – Unrelated ratios require different multipliers.

• For example, if the ratio of red marbles to blue marbles in a certain bag is $3:2$ and the ratio of white marbles to yellow marbles in that same bag is $4:5$, the ratio of red marbles to blue marbles would be $3x:2x$ and the ratio of white marbles to yellow marbles $4y:5y$.

➢ To understand why, imagine that the unknown multiplier in the first ratio is 3.

• The bag would contain 6 red marbles and 9 blue marbles. Now imagine that the unknown multiplier in the second ratio is 7. The bag would contain 28 white marbles and 35 yellow marbles.

• As you can see, **the two unknown multipliers can be different**. Since the relationship of red marbles to white marbles has nothing to do with the relationship of white marbles to yellow marbles, their respective multipliers can be different as well.

➢ Because independent ratios can have different multipliers, we must use DIFFERENT variables to represent their respective unknown multipliers.

• Although problems involving independent ratios are not particularly difficult, they are extremely RARE for the GRE. To get a sense of how to solve them, consider the following:

Bowl P contains apples and oranges in the ratio of 4 to 3 and bowl Q contains apples and oranges in the ratio of 2 to 7. Together, the two bowls contain 24 apples and 29 oranges. How many oranges does bowl P contain?

(A) 8 (B) 12 (C) 15 (D) 17 (E) 18

Answer: C. The problem states that bowl P contains apples and oranges in the ratio of $4:3$ and that bowl Q contains apples and oranges in the ratio of $2:7$. **Because the two ratios are independent, their multipliers must be different.**

$$\text{apples : oranges} \qquad \text{apples : oranges}$$
$$4x:3x \qquad\qquad 2y:7y$$

• If the two bowls contain a total of 24 apples, then $4x + 2y = 24$, as $4x$ and $2y$ represent the number of apples in bowls P and Q, respectively.

➢ Likewise, if the two bowls contain a total of 29 oranges, then $3x + 7y = 29$, since $3x$ and $7y$ represent the number of oranges in bowls P and Q.

• Thus we have two equations:

$$4x + 2y = 24 \qquad 3x + 7y = 29$$

• If we rewrite the **first equation** as $2y = 24 - 4x$ and simplify it to $y = 12 - 2x$, we can **substitute** it into the **second equation**. Doing so shows us that $x = 5$, since:

$$3x + 7y = 29$$
$$3x + 7(12 - 2x) = 29$$
$$3x + 84 - 14x = 29$$
$$-11x = -55$$
$$x = 5$$

➢ Because the number of oranges in bowl P can be represented as $3x$, bowl P must contain 15 oranges, as $3x = 3(5) = 15$.

• The correct answer is therefore (C).

(11) Overlapping Ratios – Any two ratios that share a common element can be referred to as overlapping ratios.

• To solve problems involving overlapping ratios, the two ratios must be **combined** into a single ratio.

> ➢ This can be done by determining **the least common multiple** (LCM) of the overlapped element and converting the ratios.

• To convert the ratios, simply multiply each ratio by whatever factor raises the overlapped element to the LCM. To get a sense of how this works, consider the following:

In a certain bowl of fruit, there are 9 grapes for every 2 apples and 3 apples for every 4 oranges. If the bowl contains 54 grapes, how many oranges does it contain?

(A) 12 (B) 14 (C) 15 (D) 16 (E) 18

Answer. D. The problem states that the ratio of grapes to apples is 9 : 2 and that the ratio of apples to oranges is 3 : 4. Because these ratios refer to the SAME group of apples, the ratios are not independent. They are OVERLAPPED.

To solve this problem, let's first label the ratios with the unknown multiplier. The unknown multiplier is necessary because these "part-to-part" ratios are only relative: they do not specify exact numbers.

$$\text{grapes : } \textbf{apples} \qquad \textbf{apples} \text{ : oranges}$$
$$9x : \boxed{2x} \qquad \boxed{3x} : 4x$$

Since it's IMPOSSIBLE for the same group of apples to equal both $2x$ and $3x$, we next need to multiply the first ratio by 3 and the second ratio by 2. Doing so will **raise each term to $6x$**, their least common multiple:

$$\text{grapes : apples} \qquad\qquad \text{apples : oranges}$$
$$9x : \boxed{2x} \;\rightarrow\; 27x : \boxed{6x} \qquad \boxed{3x} : 4x \;\rightarrow\; \boxed{6x} : 8x$$

Now that apples = $6x$ in both ratios, we can combine the two ratios as follows:

$$\text{grapes : apples: oranges}$$
$$27x : 6x : 8x$$

According to the problem, the bowl contains 54 grapes. Since grapes = $27x$, we know that $54 = 27x$, so the unknown multiplier must equal 2. Thus, if the bowl contains $8x$ oranges and $x = 2$, the bowl must have 16 oranges, since $8x = 8(2) = 16$.

- Here's a second example for additional practice:

In a bag of red, white, and blue marbles, the ratio of red to white marbles is 3 : 4 and the ratio of white to blue marbles is 3 : 5.

<u>**Quantity A**</u>

The least number of marbles that the bag can contain

<u>**Quantity B**</u>

If the bag were to have 42 marbles that are not blue, the number of blue marbles that it would contain

Answer: A. The problem states that the ratio of red marbles to white marbles is 3 : 4 and that the ratio of white marbles to blue marbles is 3 : 5. Since these ratios refer to the SAME group of white marbles, the ratios are OVERLAPPED.

To answer the question, let's first label the ratios with the unknown multiplier. The unknown multiplier is necessary because these "part-to-part" ratios are only relative:

red : **white**   **white** : blue

$3x : \boxed{4x}$ $\boxed{3x} : 5x$

We next need to multiply the first ratio by 3 and the second ratio by 4, since it's impossible for the same group of white marbles to equal both $4x$ and $3x$. Doing so will **raise $4x$ and $3x$ to $12x$**, their least common multiple:

red : white   white : blue

$3x : \boxed{4x} \rightarrow 9x : \boxed{12x}$ $\boxed{3x} : 5x \rightarrow \boxed{12x} : 20x$

Now that white marbles = $12x$ in both ratios, we can combine the two ratios as follows:

red : white: blue

$9x : 12x : 20x$

According to this statement, the bag has $9x + 12x + 20x = 41x$ marbles. If x equals 1, the bag has 41 marbles. If x is less than 1, the bag (impossibly) has fractional marbles, negative marbles, or no marbles at all. For example, if $x = 0.2$, the bag would have $9x = 9(0.2) = 1.8$ red marbles. Thus, **the bag has a minimum of 41 marbles**, so Quantity A is 41.

If the bag were to have 42 marbles that are not blue, it would have 42 marbles that are either red or white, since the bag only has red, white, and blue marbles. Because red marbles = $9x$ and white marbles = $12x$, we know that $9x + 12x = 42$. We can simplify this statement to $21x = 42$, proving that $x = 2$. The correct answer is therefore (A), since Quantity B is 40, as the bag would have $20x = 20(2) = $ **40 blue marbles**.

(12) Altered Ratios – Every now and then, a GRE problem will alter a ratio through the addition or subtraction of elements.

• Although altered ratio problems are RARE, they're easy to spot. Such problems always involve an initial ratio that is transformed through one or more alterations.

➢ To solve altered ratio problems, first set up the initial ratio with the UNKNOWN MULTIPLIER.

• Then and add or subtract the given changes from the ratio. The result will equal the NEW ratio, providing you with an equation you can use to solve for the unknown multiplier.

• To get a sense of how this works, consider the following:

The ratio of red marbles to blue marbles in a certain bag is 8 to 5. If 7 red marbles were to be removed from the bag and 7 blue marbles were to be added, the ratio of red marbles to blue marbles would be 5 to 4. How many red marbles does the bag currently contain?

(A) 27   (B) 48   (C) 65   (D) 72   (E) 90

Answer: D. The INITIAL ratio between the number of red marbles and the number of blue marbles is 8 to 5:

$$\frac{red}{blue} = \frac{8x}{5x} \qquad \text{initial ratio}$$

If 7 red marbles were to be removed and 7 blue marbles added, and the NEW ratio of red to blue marbles were to be 5 to 4, the relationship between the ALTERED ratio and the new ratio would be:

$$\text{altered ratio} \qquad \frac{red}{blue} : \frac{8x - 7}{5x + 7} = \frac{5}{4} \qquad \text{new ratio}$$

Cross-multiplication shows that $x = 9$, since:

$$4(8x - 7) = 5(5x + 7)$$
$$32x - 28 = 25x + 35$$
$$7x = 63$$
$$x = 9$$

Plugging $x = 9$ back into the NEW ratio reveals that the bag CURRENTLY contains 72 red marbles, since the INITIAL number of red marbles = $8x$, and $8x = 8(9) = 72$.

➤ Note that **the NEW ratio does NOT need the unknown multiplier.** Only the initial ratio requires it.

- To understand why, let's reconsider the previous problem:

$$\frac{red}{blue}: \frac{8x-7}{5x+7} = \frac{5}{4}$$

- As you may recall, **independent ratios require different multipliers.** Since the initial and new ratios do not overlap, they are unrelated and thus in need of different multipliers. As such, the relationship between them is technically:

$$\frac{red}{blue}: \frac{8x-7}{5x+7} = \frac{5\,y}{4\,y}$$

➤ Note, however, that the second multiplier is actually UNNECCESSARY: the y's cancels out.

- Since the second multiplier ALWAYS cancels in altered ratio problems, you're free to ignore it. Here's one more sample problem for you:

On farm F, the ratio of cows to goats is 1 to 5. If the farm were to add 5 more cows and 75 more goats, the ratio of cows to goats would be 1 to 7. What is the combined number of cows and goats currently at farm F?

(A) 120   (B) 144   (C) 150   (D) 165   (E) 180

Answer. A. The **initial** ratio between the number of cows and the number of goats is 1 to 5:

$$\frac{cows}{goats} = \frac{x}{5x}$$

If 5 more cows and 75 more goats were to be added, and the **new** ratio of cows to goats were to be 1 to 7, the relationship between the **altered** ratio and the new ratio would be:

$$\frac{cows}{goats}: \frac{x+5}{5x+75} = \frac{1}{7}$$

Cross-multiplication shows that $x = 20$, since:

$$7(x+5) = 1(5x+75)$$
$$7x + 35 = 5x + 75$$
$$2x = 40$$

Plugging $x = 20$ back into the **initial** ratio reveals that there is a total of 120 cows and goats currently at the farm, since the **current number of cows and goats** is x and $5x$, respectively, and $x + 5x = 6x = 6(20) = 120$.

Practice Questions

(13) Problem Sets – The following questions have been arranged into three groups: fundamental, intermediate, and rare or advanced.

• Whether you're aiming for a perfect score or a score closer to average, mastery of the concepts in the FUNDAMENTAL questions is absolutely essential.

➤ As you might expect, the INTERMEDIATE questions are more difficult but are essential for test-takers who need an above-average score or higher.

• Finally, the RARE or ADVANCED questions test concepts that are very sophisticated or seldom encountered on the GRE. Mastery of such questions is required only if you need a math score above the 90th percentile.

• As always, if you find yourself confused, bogged down with busy work, or stuck, don't be afraid to fall back on your "Plan B" strategies!

Fundamental

1. Simplify each of the following ratios:

    a. 1.4 to 2   b. $\frac{1}{4}:\frac{4}{9}$

    c. $1\frac{1}{2}$ to $2\frac{2}{3}$ d. $\left(\frac{1}{2}\right)^3$ to $\left(\frac{1}{4}\right)^2$

2. For every 5 English majors at a certain university, there are 9 students who are not English majors. What is the ratio of the total number of students at the university to the total number of students who are English majors?

$$\text{(A) } \frac{5}{14} \quad \text{(B) } \frac{9}{14} \quad \text{(C) } \frac{14}{9} \quad \text{(D) } \frac{2}{1} \quad \text{(E) } \frac{14}{5}$$

$$2a = 7b$$
$$ab \neq 0$$

Quantity A	Quantity B
The ratio of a to b	The ratio of b to a

3.

4. At noon on a clear day, a 20-foot statue casts a shadow 16 feet long. At the same time on the same day, a nearby statue casts a shadow 20 feet long. If the lengths of the shadows are proportional to the heights of the statues, what is the length, in feet, of the taller statue?

(A) 22 (B) 23 (C) 24 (D) 25 (E) 26

5. If the degree measures of the angles of a quadrilateral add to 360° and are in the ratio 3 : 4 : 5 : 8, what is the degree measure of the largest angle?

(A) 90° (B) 100° (C) 120° (D) 130° (E) 144°

6. If 12 cupcakes cost a total of $9.60, then at this rate, what is the cost of 10 cupcakes?

(A) $7.80 (B) $8.00 (C) $8.25 (D) $8.60 (E) $8.85

7. If 6 office workers, working non-stop at uniform rates, can complete a certain project in 12 hours, how long would it take 8 office workers, working non-stop at identical uniform rates, to complete the same project?

```
┌─────────────┐
│             │
└─────────────┘
```

8. A watch gains 10 minutes and 44 seconds every 7 days. If the rate of gain is constant, how much does the watch gain in one day?

(A) 1 min 12 sec (B) 1 min 24 sec (C) 1 min 32 sec (D) 1 min 40 sec (E) 1 min 48 sec

A certain recipe requires 9/2 cups of flour and makes 1 dozen muffins. (1 dozen = 12)

	Quantity A	Quantity B
9.	The amount of flour required for the same recipe to make 18 muffins	6 cups

10. When walking, a certain person takes 18 complete steps in 10 seconds. At this rate, how many complete steps does the person take in 52 seconds?

(A) 67 (B) 72 (C) 78 (D) 85 (E) 93

Intermediate

11. Simplify each of the following ratios:

    a. $\dfrac{1}{2}:\dfrac{2}{3}:\dfrac{3}{4}$ b. 0.12 to 5 to 2.4

    c. $\dfrac{p}{q}$ to its reciprocal   d. $0.15:\dfrac{2}{5}:\dfrac{3}{4}$

In May, the ratio of men to women at company C was 7 to 17. During the month, 3 additional men and 3 additional women were hired by company C, and nobody left the company or was fired.

Quantity A	Quantity B

12.   The ratio of men to women in company C at the end of the month $\dfrac{1}{2}$

13. Bill eats apples, bananas, and cantaloupes in the ratio of $4:7:5$. If Bill eats 6 more bananas than cantaloupes, how many apples did he eat?

For each house in Town T, the amount of property tax is x percent of the value of the house. The property tax on a house whose value is \$450,000 is \$12,000.

Quantity A	Quantity B

14.   The property tax on a house in Town T whose value is \$540,000   \$13,000

$$a - b + c = 0$$
$$3a + b + 4c = 0$$

15. In the system of equations above, if $abc \neq 0$, then the ratio of a to c is

    (A) $-\dfrac{3}{2}$ (B) $-\dfrac{5}{4}$ (C) $-\dfrac{2}{3}$ (D) $\dfrac{4}{5}$ (E) $\dfrac{5}{4}$

A single sheet of paper weighs 0.002 pounds,
and 600 sheets of paper cost $9.00.

	Quantity A	Quantity B
16.	The cost, in dollars, of a stack of paper weighing 0.18 pounds	$1.25

17. A 36-inch ruler is marked off in eighteenths of an inch. What is the distance, in inches, from the zero mark to the 107th mark after the zero mark?

$$\text{(A) } 5\frac{7}{9} \quad \text{(B) } 5\frac{17}{18} \quad \text{(C) } 6\frac{4}{9} \quad \text{(D) } 6\frac{5}{6} \quad \text{(E) } 7\frac{1}{3}$$

A class of x boys and girls contains exactly y girls. $(y \neq 0)$.

	Quantity A	Quantity B
18.	The ratio of the number of boys in the class to the number of girls in the class.	$\frac{x}{y} - 1$

19. Leia has exactly 5 times as many pennies as nickels in her coin collection. If Leia's coin collection only contains pennies and nickels, which of the following CANNOT be the number of coins in the collection?

(A) 96   (B) 84   (C) 72   (D) 64   (E) 54

20. On farm F, there are 3/4 as many goats as pigs, 2/5 as many chickens as goats, and twice as many chickens as sheep. What is the ratio of sheep to pigs on farm F?

$$\text{(A) } \frac{3}{20} \quad \text{(B) } \frac{2}{7} \quad \text{(C) } \frac{3}{5} \quad \text{(D) } \frac{5}{4} \quad \text{(E) } \frac{6}{5}$$

Rare or Advanced

21. In a certain bag of marbles, the ratio of reds to whites is 3 : 4 and the ratio of whites to blues is 3 : 5. If the bag contains 64 marbles that are either white or blue, how many reds does the bag contain?

    ☐

22. A certain task force has an equal number of men and women. If 2 men and 1 woman were to quit the force, the ratio of men to women on the force would be 7 to 8. How many men would the task force have if the 2 men were to quit?

    (A) 7   (B) 8   (C) 9   (D) 10   (E) 12

23. A jar of nuts contains almonds, cashews, and pecans, and nothing else. If the ratio of almonds to cashews is 2 to 3, and the ratio of cashews to pecans is 1 to 2, then the total number of nuts in the jar can equal which of the following?

    Indicate all such numbers.

    [A] 55   [B] 80   [C] 99   [D] 110   [E] 132

24. If 5 model-X machines working independently can make a combined total of 5 computer chips in 5 minutes, then 20 model-X machines working independently can produce a combined total of 20 computer chips in exactly how many minutes?

    (A) 4 min   (B) 5 min   (C) 8 min   (D) 10 min   (E) 20 min

25. The ratio of red to white marbles in Ari's marble collection is 2 to 3, and the ratio of red to white marbles in Maia's marble collection is 1 to 4. If Ari and Maia have 40 red marbles and 70 white marbles, collectively, how many white marbles does Maia have?

    (A) 4   (B) 16   (C) 18   (D) 36   (E) 54

26. Lot S has trucks, sedans, and coupes such that the ratio of trucks to sedans is 3 to 5 and the ratio of sedans to coupes is 6 to 5. Lot T has trucks and sedans in the ratio of 16 to 29. If the two lots have 440 sedans, collectively, how many trucks does lot T have?

    (A) 80   (B) 100   (C) 120   (D) 140   (E) 160

(14) Solutions – Video solutions for each of the previous questions can be found on our website at **www.sherpaprep.com/videos**.

• BOOKMARK this address for future visits!

   ➤ To view the videos, you'll need the LOGIN and PASSWORD that you created upon registering your copy of Word Problems.

• If you have yet to register your book yet, please go to **www.sherpaprep.com/activate** and enter your email address, last name, and shipping address.

• Be sure to provide the SAME last name and shipping address that you used to purchase your copy of Master Key to the GRE or to enroll in your GRE course with Sherpa Prep!

   ➤ When checking your answers, we encourage you to watch the solution for any problem that you answered INCORRECTLY

• The same goes for any problem that took you MORE than TWO MINUTES to solve.

• After digesting the explanation, REVISIT your mistake a couple of days later to ensure that the problem no longer poses issues to you.

   ➤ If you struggle to solve the problem a SECOND time, add it to your "LOG of ERRORS" and redo it every few weeks.

• Solving tricky questions MORE THAN ONCE is the best way to learn from your mistakes and to avoid similar difficulties on your actual exam.

Fundamental		Intermediate		Rare or Advanced
1a. 7/10	8. C	11a. 6:8:9	18. C	21. 18
1b. 9/16	9. A	11b. 3:125:60	19. D	22. A
1c. 9/16	10. E	11c. $p^2 : q^2$	20. A	23. A, C, D, E
1d. 2		11d. 3:8:15		24. B
2. E		12. D		25. B
3. A		13. 12		26. E
4. D		14. A		
5. E		15. B		
6. B		16. A		
7. 9		17. B		

Rates

Rates

To be discussed:

Fundamental Concepts

Whether you're aiming for a perfect score or a score closer to average, mastery of the following concepts is essential.

1	Introduction
2	Using Rate Tables
3	Quantity Cost Problems
4	Proportions
5	Converting Units
6	Working Together Problems
7	Geometric Rates
8	Asswholes

Rare or Advanced Concepts

The following concepts are either advanced or are tested only on rare occasions. If you don't need an elite math score, don't waste your time!

9	Travelers & Trips
10	Altered Rates
11	The Average Rate Trap
12	Exponential Growth

Practice Questions & Drills

There's no substitute for elbow grease. Practice your new skills to ensure that you internalize what you've studied.

13	Problem Sets
14	Solutions

Fundamental Concepts

(1) Introduction – Any problem that involves the interplay of a rate, a quantity, and an output can be referred to as a rate problem.

• There are several challenges to solving rate problems. One big one is that they're not always easy to identify. Consider the following question:

> **"How long will it take John to type x words if he types y words per minute?"**

> ➤ At first glance, you might not recognize that this is a rate problem. For starters, the word "rate" is nowhere to be seen.

• A RATE, however, is simply a relationship that compares two different units.

• Thus, when a problem mentions **an "x per y" relationship** — such as "y words per minute" — it involves a rate, since these sorts of phrases compare different units. Hence:

"Dollars per Item"		"Miles per Hour"
Compares dollars to tickets		Compares miles to hours

> ➤ You might also fail to recognize the question above as a rate problem, since it doesn't appear to involve any quantities.

• In the context of a rate problem, a QUANTITY is the number of people (or objects) working at the rate.

• For example, if a problem mentions that "6 workers each earn $15 per hour", that problem has a quantity of 6 workers.

> ➤ A quantity, however, can also be thought of as a length of TIME during which a person (or object) works.

• Thus, in the question above, the quantity is the unknown number of minutes it takes John to type x words.

• On the GRE, **most rate problems involve a quantity of time**. Although other sorts of quantities do appear, the majority of examples pertain to a person (or object) working for a certain span of time.

➢ The OUTPUT produced by a person (or object) working at a certain rate is commonly known as WORK.

• WORK can be thought of as anything that is produced, performed, or earned.

• For example, a hammer, a job, or a sum of money can all be considered examples of work, since a hammer is manufactured, a job is performed, and money is earned.

➢ Work can ALSO be thought of as a DISTANCE traveled. Imagine a jogger who travels at a rate of 6 miles per hour for two hours.

• When the two hours are up, he or she has "produced" a 12-mile run. Thus, his or her work would equal 12 miles.

• On the GRE, **roughly half of all rate problems involve distance**. So if you encounter a problem in which a person or object travels a distance, remember that distance equals work!

➢ The relationship between a rate, a quantity, and work can be summarized with the following formula, which (naturally) we call the RATE FORMULA:

Rate × Quantity (e.g. Time) = Work

• In the problem at the top of the previous page, we are asked how long it will take John to type x words if he types y words a minute.

• Since John will type x words, that is the **work** he will produce. Likewise, if he will type y words per minute, that is the **rate** at which he will do the work.

➢ It's unclear, of course, how long it will take John to do this work, but we can let T = the **time** it will take him to do so.

• If we insert this information into the rate formula we get the following equation:

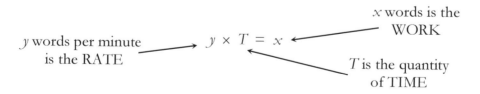

$$y \text{ words per minute is the RATE} \qquad y \times T = x \qquad \begin{array}{l} x \text{ words is the WORK} \\ T \text{ is the quantity of TIME} \end{array}$$

• Thus, the time it will take John to type x words will equal $\frac{x}{y}$, since we can divide both sides of this equation by y to solve for T, like so:

$$y \times T = x \quad \rightarrow \quad T = \frac{x}{y}$$

(2) Using Rate Tables – In many cases, the easiest way to solve a rate problem is with the rate formula.

• When doing so, we strongly encourage you to set up a RATE TABLE. Rate tables are a great way to organize relevant information and to establish important equations.

➤ To set up a Rate Table, first WRITE DOWN the rate formula. For many problems, the version of the formula that you'll need will be: RATE × TIME = WORK.

• To save time, you can abbreviate this as R × T = W. If your problem involves a distance, you can write R × T = D instead.

• Then DRAW a LINE beneath the formula, like so:

$$\begin{array}{ccccc} \mathbf{R} & \times & \mathbf{T} & = & \mathbf{W} \\ \hline ??? & \times & ??? & = & ??? \end{array}$$

The RATE TABLE

➤ Once your table has been drawn, ENTER any information you've been given BENEATH the appropriate variables.

• For example, imagine that you were asked "**how many hours will it take a train to travel 12n miles at the rate of 2n/3 miles per hour?**"

• Since the train will travel a DISTANCE of 12n miles at a RATE of 2n/3 miles per hour (remember, "*x* per *y*" phrases are <u>always</u> rates), we know that:

The rate is 2n/3 miles per hour

$$\begin{array}{ccccc} \mathbf{R} & \times & \mathbf{T} & = & \mathbf{D} \\ \hline \frac{2n}{3} & \times & ??? & = & 12n \end{array}$$

The distance is 12n miles

➤ Finally, use the EQUATION in your table to solve for this missing piece of information.

• Here, we don't know how many hours it will take the train, so we can let *t* = TIME. Doing so gives us:

$$\frac{2n}{3} \times t = 12n$$

The unknown time is *t* hours.

• Multiplying both sides of the equation by $\frac{3}{2n}$ tells us that the train took 18 hours, since:

$$t = 12n \times \frac{3}{2n} \quad \rightarrow \quad t = {}^{6}\cancel{12n} \times \frac{3}{\cancel{2n}} = 18 \text{ hrs}$$

- To give you a better feel for using Rate Tables, consider the following:

Quantity A   **Quantity B**

The time required to travel n miles at p miles per hour

The time required to travel $2n$ miles at $\frac{p}{3}$ miles per hour

Answer: B. In the case of Quantity A, we know that the **distance** traveled will be n miles and that the **rate** of travel will be p miles per hour. Plugging this information into a Rate Table gives us:

R	×	T	=	D
p	×	???	=	n

If we let $t =$ the unknown **time**, we can use this equation to solve for t by dividing both sides by p:

$$p \times t = n \quad \rightarrow \quad t = \frac{n}{p}$$

➤ In the case of Quantity B, we know that the **distance** traveled will be $2n$ miles and that the **rate** of travel will be $\frac{p}{3}$ miles per hour.

- Plugging this information into a Rate Table gives us:

R	×	T	=	D
$\frac{p}{3}$	×	???	=	$2n$

If we let $t =$ the unknown **time**, we can use this equation to solve for t by multiplying both sides by $\frac{3}{p}$:

$$\frac{p}{3} \times t = 2n \quad \rightarrow \quad t = 2n \times \frac{3}{p} = \frac{6n}{p}$$

- Because **distance and time are inherently positive**, and $r \times t = d$, the rate must also be positive.

➤ Therefore, n and p must represent positive numbers. As such, we can use the Comparison Trick to compare these fractions:

Quantity A   Quantity B

np $6np$

$\dfrac{n}{p} \quad \overset{}{\bowtie} \quad \dfrac{6n}{p}$

- Quantity B must be greater than Quantity A, since $6np$ is larger than np when n and p are positive. Thus, the correct answer is (B).

> ➢ For some rate problems, you may need to use the Rate Table TWICE.

• Typically, in such cases, you need to determine one piece of information in order to solve for a second. Consider the following:

A gopher takes 6 minutes to dig $\frac{3}{11}$ of a tunnel. At this rate, how many minutes will it take the gopher to complete the rest of the tunnel?

(A) 12   (B) 14   (C) 15   (D) 16   (E) 17

Answer. D. According to the problem, the gopher has dug 3/11 of a tunnel, so 8/11 of the tunnel awaits completion.

> ➢ To determine how long this will take, however, we need to know the rate at which the gopher digs.

• We've been told that it takes the gopher 6 minutes to dig 3/11 of a tunnel. Since 6 minutes is a **time** and 3/11 of the tunnel is the **work** the gopher has performed, we can use this information to determine his rate.

R	×	T	=	W
r	×	6	=	$\frac{3}{11}$

If we let r = **rate**, our Rate Table tells us that the gopher digs at a rate of 1/22 of a tunnel per minute, since:

$$r = \frac{\cancel{3}}{11} \times \frac{1}{\cancel{6}_2} = \frac{1}{22}$$

> ➢ Thus, if the gopher digs at a **rate** of 1/22 of a tunnel per minute, and still has to complete 8/11 of the **work**, we can use a second Rate Table to determine how long this will take.

R	×	T	=	W
$\frac{1}{22}$	×	t	=	$\frac{8}{11}$

If we let t = **time**, we can solve for t as follows:

$$t = \frac{8}{\cancel{11}} \times \frac{\cancel{22}^2}{1} = 16$$

• Therefore, it will take the gopher 16 minutes to complete 8/11 of the tunnel if the gopher digs at its current rate. Hence, the correct answer is (D).

(3) Quantity Cost Problems – GRE rates problems often involve the interplay of quantity and cost.

• From a mathematical standpoint, such problems are no different than other rate problems, even though they don't involve time.

> ➤ You may find it's easier, however, to think of them as Quantity Cost problems, since many examples DON'T use the word RATE.

• To solve them, simply use the formula below instead of the regular rate formula. Although the two formulas are really one and the same, the headings "quantity" and "cost" may help you organize information (and your thoughts) more effectively.

Rate × Quantity = Cost or Distance

• Consider the following:

Monica drove a total of 810 miles on a personal vacation. If her car averaged 27 miles per gallon of gasoline, and gasoline cost her an average of $2.25 per gallon, how much did she spend, in dollars, on gasoline during her vacation?

(A) 60 (B) 62.50 (C) 65 (D) 67.50 (E) 70

Answer. D. In order to calculate how much Monica spent on gas during her vacation, we first need to determine how much gas she used.

R	×	Q	=	D
27	×	q	=	810

If she drove a **distance** of 810 miles at an average **rate** of 27 miles per gallon (remember, "x per y" phrases are always rates), she consumed 30 gallons of gas, since:

$$q = \frac{810}{27} = \frac{\cancel{9}(90)}{\cancel{9}(3)} = 30$$

• If the **rate** of gasoline was $2.25 per gallon, and 30 gallons of gas were used, then the correct answer is (D), since the cost of the gas must have been $67.50:

R	×	Q	=	C
2.25	×	30	=	???

$$2.25 \times 30 = 22.5 \times 3 = 66 + 1.5 = 67.5$$

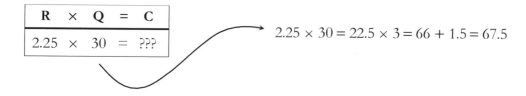

Sherpa
Prep

(4) Proportions – Some rate problems can also be solved with proportions.

- In general, such problems tend to be fairly basic and can always be solved with the rate formula instead.

  ➢ You may find it EASIER, however, to solve them as "apples-to-oranges" proportions.

- To ensure that you do so correctly, LABEL each item within the proportion. Then cross-multiply to solve the equation.

- Consider the following:

Running at the same constant rate, 9 identical machines can produce a total of 150 books every hour. At this rate, how many books could 15 such machines produce in 3 hours?

(A) 250   (B) 750   (C) 1,250   (D) 2,250   (E) 58,500

Answer: B. According to the problem, 9 machines can produce 150 books in one hour. Since the relationship between machines and books is an "apples-to-oranges" relationship, we can use the following proportion to determine how many books 15 machines could produce in 1 hour:

$$\frac{9 \text{ machines}}{150 \text{ books}} = \frac{15 \text{ machines}}{x \text{ books}}$$

- If we cross-multiply, we get $x = 250$:

$$9x = 15(150) \rightarrow x = \frac{15(150)}{9} = \frac{15(150)}{3(3)} = 5(50) = 250$$

- Thus, if 15 machines can produce 250 books in 1 hour, they should produce 750 books in 3 hours, since $250 \times 3 = 750$, which is answer (B).

  ➢ But be CAREFUL. If you like using proportions to solve rate problems, you've got to remember that some relationships are INVERSE.

- As mentioned in our discussion of Ratios & Proportions, any relationship in which one quantity increases while the other quantity decreases is INVERSELY proportional.

- An example of such a relationship would be that between RATE and TIME, since the time it takes to travel a certain distance **decreases** as a traveler's rate **increases**.

  ➤ You CANNOT use traditional proportions to solve rate problems with inverse relationships.

- To solve such problems, you must SET the PRODUCTS of the two quantities EQUAL to one another. If you use a proportion to solve an inverse relationship, your solution will be wrong.

- Consider the following:

If 4 machines, working non-stop at uniform rates, can complete a certain task in 144 seconds, how many seconds would it take 9 machines, working non-stop at identical uniform rates, to complete the same task?

(A) 48 (B) 64 (C) 81 (D) 216 (E) 324

Answer: B. Because the amount of time needed to complete a task should **decrease** as the number of machines **increases**, the relationship between time and machines is inversely proportional.

  ➤ To solve this problem, therefore, we need to set the **product** of 4 machines × 144 seconds equal to the **product** of 9 machines × *s* seconds:

$$4 \text{ machines} \times 144 \text{ seconds} = 9 \text{ machines} \times s \text{ seconds}$$
$$4(144) = 9s$$
$$s = \frac{4(144)}{9} = \frac{4(12)(12)}{3(3)} = 4(4)(4) = 64$$

- Since it would take 9 machines 64 seconds to complete the task, the correct answer is therefore (B). If we were to solve this problem with a traditional proportion, we would set up the relationship between machines and books like this:

increases

$$\frac{4 \text{ machines}}{144 \text{ seconds}} = \frac{9 \text{ machines}}{x \text{ seconds}}$$

increases

We CANNOT use a proportion to solve this problem.

- But this would be WRONG: it implies that 9 machines would take MORE time to complete the task than 4 machines. This does not pass a reasonable person's "sanity check".

(5) Converting Units – In rate problems, it is critical that the units of the rate match those elsewhere in the problem.

- If the units are MISMATCHED, e.g. if the rate of a jogger is expressed in **meters** per second but his or her distance is required in **kilometers**, the units must be ALIGNED.

  ➤ To align the units of a particular rate, time, or distance, first identify the CONVERSION FACTOR of the mismatched units.

- The conversion factor expresses the precise relationship between the two units.

- For example, the conversion factor between inches and feet is **12 inches = 1 foot**, since there are 12 inches in 1 foot. Likewise, the conversion factor between minutes and seconds is **1 minute = 60 seconds**, since 1 minute contains 60 seconds.

  ➤ The ONLY conversion factors that you are expected to know are the units of TIME, such as the minutes in an hour, and the METRIC units provided below.

- You do NOT need to know the conversion factors for yards, miles, inches, feet, ounces, or other non-metric measurements.

Units of TIME | METRIC Units

1 year = 365 days, 12 months, 52 weeks | 1 kilometer = 1,000 meters
1 week = 7 days | 1 meter = 100 centimeters
1 day = 24 hours | 1 centimeter = 10 millimeters

- Should a question require other conversion factors, it will provide them for you.

  ➤ Once you've identified the appropriate conversion factor, set up an "apples to oranges" PROPORTION to align the units.

- To ensure that you do so correctly, LABEL each unit within the proportion. Hence, if **1,000 meters = 1 kilometer**, you can convert 3 meters into kilometers as follows:

$$\frac{1,000 \text{ meters}}{1 \text{ kilometers}} = \frac{3 \text{ meters}}{x \text{ kilometers}}$$

- Finally, cross-multiply to solve. Thus, 3 meters = 0.003 kilometers, since:

$$1,000x = 3 \quad \rightarrow \quad x = \frac{3}{1,000} = 0.003 \text{ kilometers}$$

➤ When solving a problem with MISTMATCHED units, be sure to WRITE the units in your Rate Table so that you can SEE the mismatch.

• Then align them before solving the problem. Once aligned, the units can be IGNORED. Ignoring the units will remove the clutter from your equation, making it easier to solve.

• Consider the following:

The Sun is roughly 150 million kilometers from Earth, and light from the Sun travels to Earth at the rate of approximately 300,000 kilometers per second. Approximately how many <u>minutes</u> does it take for light to travel from the Sun to Earth?

(A) 8 (B) 14 (C) 16 (D) 28 (E) 32

Answer: A. According to the problem, the <u>distance</u> from the Sun to the Earth is 150,000,000 kilometers, and light travels at a <u>rate</u> of approximately 300,000 kilometers per second.

Here, time is in   **R × T = D**   Here, time is in
SECONDS   MINUTES

$$\frac{300{,}000 \text{ km}}{1 \text{ sec}} \times t \text{ min} = 150{,}000{,}000 \text{ km}$$

➤ However, the provided units are mismatched: the rate is given in terms of **seconds**, but the time is required in **minutes**.

• **To end up with a time in minutes, we need to convert seconds to minutes.** Since 60 seconds = 1 minute, we know that 1 second = 1/60 of a minute. Thus, we can adjust our Rate Table, like so:

$1 \text{ sec} = \frac{1}{60} \text{ min}$

R × T = D

$$\frac{300{,}000 \text{ km}}{\frac{1}{60} \text{ min}} \times t \text{ min} = 150{,}000{,}000 \text{ km}$$

➤ Now that our units are aligned, we can ignore them and solve for *t*. To simplify the rate, we can multiply its top by the "flip" of its bottom, giving us 300,000 × 60.

• Thus, $300{,}000 \times 60 \times t = 150{,}000{,}000$. Finally, if we divide both sides by $300{,}000 \times 60$, and cancel the 6 zeroes in common on top and on bottom, we get:

$$t = \frac{150{,}000{,}000}{300{,}000(60)} = \frac{\cancel{150}^{\,50}}{\cancel{3}(6)} = \frac{50}{6} = 8\frac{1}{3}$$

Since $8\frac{1}{3}$ is approximately 8, the correct answer must be (A).

> ➤ If you have to convert SQUARED or CUBIC units, we strongly encourage you to do so at the OUTSET of your problem.

• Performing other operations before aligning such units can sometimes cause problems. Consider the following:

A rectangular wall 6 feet wide and 15 feet tall is to be painted. It takes Celinda 1 minute to paint 2 square yards. (1 yard = 3 feet)

Quantity A	**Quantity B**
The time, in minutes, it will take to paint the entire wall	15 minutes

Answer: B. The area of a rectangle equals its width × its height, so the area of the wall = 6 ft × 15 ft = 90 ft². Because Celinda paints at a rate of 2 yd² per minute, it's tempting to assume that she can paint the entire wall in 15 minutes.

> ➤ After all, if 3 ft = 1 yd, then 90 ft² would seem to equal 30 yd², giving us the following Rate Table:

$$\begin{array}{ccccc} \textbf{R} & \times & \textbf{T} & = & \textbf{W} \\ \hline \dfrac{2\text{ yd}^2}{1\text{ min}} & \times & t\text{ min} & = & 30\text{ yd}^2 \end{array}$$

This Rate Table is a mistake!

• However, 90 ft² does not equal 30 yd², since the conversion rate 3 ft = 1 yd only converts feet to yards, NOT <u>square</u> feet to <u>square</u> yards.

> ➤ **By converting feet to yards at the start of the problem**, it can be shown that it will take Celinda 5 minutes to paint the entire wall.

• 6 ft = 2 yd, and 15 ft = 5 yd, so the area of the wall is 2 yd × 5 yd = 10 yd².

$$\begin{array}{ccccc} \textbf{R} & \times & \textbf{T} & = & \textbf{W} \\ \hline \dfrac{2\text{ yd}^2}{1\text{ min}} & \times & t\text{ min} & = & 10\text{ yd}^2 \end{array}$$

This Rate Table is correct.

• Thus, the correct answer is (B), since Quantity B must be larger than Quantity A if $t = 5$ min:

$$2 \times t = 10 \quad \rightarrow \quad t = \frac{10}{2} = 5 \text{ min}$$

(6) Working Together Problems – In "Working Together" problems, people (or objects) work together at DIFFERENT rates on a certain task.

• Such problems can seem intimidating (and are often confused with inverse proportion problems in which everyone works at a UNIFORM rate), but they are not much different than rate problems involving a single person (or object).

> ➢ To solve them, first set up a Working Together Table, in which the top row represents the rate, time, and work of the FIRST worker.

• Beneath this, place a row representing the rate, time, and work of the SECOND worker. If your problem has more than 2 workers, create additional rows.

	R × T = W
Worker 1	
Worker 2	
Together	

• At the bottom of the table, place a TOGETHER row that tracks the rate, time, and work of the two parties when they work together.

> ➢ The together row does NOT represent the TOTAL of the workers rates, times, or work. It merely catalogs what happens when the parties work TOGETHER.

• The benefit of a Working Together Table is twofold.

• On the one hand, it organizes data, making information easier to manage. On the other, it helps reveal relationships that might otherwise be missed.

> ➢ Once you've entered the data of the individual workers, **ADD the rates of the working parties**. This is almost always the KEY to solving these sorts of problems.

• We ADD the rates of the working parties because they are working together. EACH party is contributing to the task at hand, so the TOTAL rate of work reflects the efforts of BOTH parties.

• To get a sense of how the table works, consider the following:

Sarah, working independently at a constant rate, can do a certain job in 3 hours. Trevor, working independently at a different constant rate, can do the same job three times in 5 hours. How long would it take Sarah and Trevor, working together at their respective constant rates, to do 2/3 of a job?

(A) $\frac{1}{6}$　(B) $\frac{3}{14}$　(C) $\frac{3}{5}$　(D) $\frac{5}{7}$　(E) $\frac{8}{9}$

Answer: D. According to the problem, Sarah, working alone, can do a job **one time** in 3 hours. Trevor, working alone, can do the same job **three times** in 5 hours. We can enter this information into a Working Together Table as follows:

	R	×	T	=	W
Sarah	???	×	3	=	1
Trevor	???	×	5	=	3
Together					

➢ Thus, Sarah's rate = 1/3 of a job per hour, since she can do 1 job in 3 hours, and Trevor's rate = 3/5 of a job per hour, since he can do 3 jobs in 5 hours.

• If we ADD Sarah and Trevor's rates, we learn that **they work together at a rate of 14/15** job per hour, since:

Don't forget our FAST FRACTION SHORTCUT!　$\longrightarrow$　$\frac{1}{3}+\frac{3}{5}=\frac{(1\cdot5)+(3\cdot3)}{3\cdot5}=\frac{14}{15}$　Cross-multiply and place the SUM over the PRODUCT of the denominators.

• Hence, to determine how long it will take Sarah and Trevor to complete 2/3 of a job if they work together, we can fill out the TOGETHER row of their table as follows:

	R	×	T	=	W
Sarah	1/3	×	3	=	1
Trevor	3/5	×	5	=	3
Together	14/15	×	???	=	2/3

• If we let t = the **time** that Sarah and Trevor work together, then $\frac{14}{15}\times t=\frac{2}{3}$. Thus, the correct answer is (D), since it will take them 5/7 of an hour to complete 2/3 of a job:

$$\frac{14}{15}\times t=\frac{2}{3}\;\rightarrow\;t=\frac{2}{3}\times\frac{15}{14}=\frac{5}{7}$$

➤ In some Working Together Problems, you may notice that the workers actually WORK AGAINST one another.

• For example, one pipe may fill a tank and another may drain it. To solve such problems, **SUBTRACT the rates** of the working parties. Each party is contributing to the task at hand, so the NET rate of work must reflect the efforts of BOTH parties.

• Consider the following:

Water flows into an empty drum at spout A and out of the drum at spout B. If spout A can fill the empty drum in 4 hours and spout B can empty the drum, when full, in 7 hours, how many hours does it take both spouts to fill 3/7 of the drum?

$$\text{(A) } 3\tfrac{4}{7} \quad \text{(B) } 4 \quad \text{(C) } 4\tfrac{2}{5} \quad \text{(D) } 5 \quad \text{(E) } 5\tfrac{3}{4}$$

Answer: B. According to the problem, spout A can *fill* the drum, if empty, **once** in 4 hours and spout B can *empty* the same drum, if full, **once** in 7 hours. Thus, the rate of spout $A =$ 1/4 and the rate of spout $B = 1/7$, since 1 job ÷ 4 hours = 1/4 and 1 job ÷ 7 hours = 1/7.

	R	×	T	=	W
Spout A	1/4	×	4	=	1
Spout B	1/7	×	7	=	1
Together					

➤ Because spouts A and B are working at OPPOSITE purposes, we need to SUBTRACT their rates to determine the rate at which they work together:

$$\frac{1}{4} - \frac{1}{7} = \frac{(1\cdot 7)-(1\cdot 4)}{4\cdot 7} = \frac{3}{28}$$

• Finally, to determine how long it will take spouts A and B, working together, to fill 3/7 of an empty drum, we can set up the TOGETHER row of their table as follows:

	R	×	T	=	W
Spout A	1/4	×	4	=	1
Spout B	1/7	×	7	=	1
Together	3/28	×	t	=	3/7

• Thus, the correct answer is (B), since it takes both spouts 4 hours to fill 3/7 of the drum:

$$\frac{3}{28} \times t = \frac{3}{7} \quad \rightarrow \quad t = \frac{3}{7} \times \frac{28}{3} = 4$$

(7) Geometric Rates – On occasion, rate problems involve a bit of Geometry.

• In most cases, such problems involve CIRCLES. To solve problems involving circular distances, you'll need to remember two things:

> ➤ First, EVERY time a circle completes a REVOLUTION, a point on the edge of that circle travels the length of its CIRCUMFERENCE.

• For example, if a circle has a circumference of 9π inches, a point on the edge of that circle will travel 9π inches every time that circle rotates all the way around.

• Second, the circumference of a circle is $2\pi r$, where $\pi \approx 3.14$ and $r =$ the radius. Thus, if a point on the edge of a circle is 7 inches from the center, that point travels $2\pi(7) = 14\pi$ inches every time the circle completes a revolution, since the radius of the circle is 7 inches.

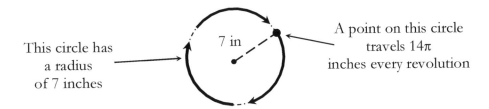

This circle has a radius of 7 inches

7 in

A point on this circle travels 14π inches every revolution

> ➤ For a complete discussion of circumference, π, and, radius, be sure to read the CIRCLES section of our book on GEOMETRY.

• If you're okay with the circumference formula, consider the following:

Point K lies on the edge of a wheel that has a radius of 4 inches. What is the distance, in inches, traveled by point K if the wheel rotates at a rate of 45 revolutions per minute for 2 minutes?

(A) 360π (B) 450π (C) 540π (D) 630π (E) 720π

Answer. E. If point K lies on the edge of a wheel with a radius of 4 inches, then the wheel has a circumference of 8π inches, since $2\pi r = 2\pi(4) = 8\pi$. Therefore, every time the wheel completes a revolution, point K travels a distance of 8π inches.

> ➤ Further, if the wheel rotates at a rate of 45 revolutions per minute, then it rotates 90 times in 2 minutes, since $45 \times 2 = 90$.

• Point K must therefore travel 720π inches in 2 minutes, since 90 revolutions of 8π inches equals $90 \times 8\pi = 720\pi$ inches. Thus, the correct answer is (E).

> Every now and then, rate problems also involve the volume of three-dimensional shapes. To solve such problems, simply let WORK = VOLUME.

• If the shape is a RECTANGULAR SOLID, its volume will equal the product of its length, width, and height. Consider the following:

An empty swimming pool is filled with water at a constant rate of 48 cubic feet per hour. If the pool is 20 feet long and 12 feet wide, and has a uniform depth of 12 feet, approximately how many hours will it take to fill the pool?

(A) 24   (B) 36   (C) 48   (D) 60   (E) 72

Answer: D. Since the pool is filled with water at a **rate** of 48 ft^3/hr and its **volume** equals the product of its length, width, and height (in this case, depth), our Rate Table should be:

$$\underline{\quad R \times T = V \quad}$$
$$48 \times t = 20 \times 12 \times 12$$

• Thus, the correct answer is (D), since it will take 60 hours to fill the pool:

$$t = \frac{20 \times 12 \times 12}{48} = \frac{20 \times 12 \times \cancel{12}}{4 \times \cancel{12}} = 20 \times 3 = 60 \text{ hrs}$$

> If the shape is a CYLINDER, its volume will equal $\pi r^2 h$, where r represents the radius of the cylinder and h the height.

• Consider the following:

Tank T is a cylinder that, when empty, takes exactly 8 minutes to fill at a constant rate of 0.3 cubic inches per second. What is the volume, in cubic inches, of tank T?

(A) 96   (B) 108   (C) 124   (D) 136   (E) 144

Answer: E. Tank T is filled at a **rate** of 0.3 in^3/sec. In terms of minutes, this rate should equal 18 in^3/min, since 1 second = 1/60 of a minute:

$$\frac{0.3 \text{ in}^3}{1 \text{ sec}} = \frac{0.3 \text{ in}^3}{\frac{1}{60} \text{ min}} = 0.3 \times 60 = 3 \times 6 = \frac{18 \text{ in}^3}{\text{min}}$$

• If tank T takes 8 **minutes** to fill at a rate of 18 in^3/min, then the correct answer is (E), since its volume = 144 in^3:

$$\underline{\quad R \times T = V \quad}$$
$$\frac{18 \text{ in}^3}{\text{min}} \times 8 \text{ min} = 144 \text{ in}^3$$

(8) Asswholes – Like Algebraic Word Problems, Rate Problems are often "Asswholes".

• Remember, any problem that contains VARIABLES in its ANSWER CHOICES can be solved in either of two ways: algebraically or by assigning numbers.

➢ While most Asswholes are easier to solve by assigning numbers, feel free to solve them algebraically if you are CERTAIN that you can do the work.

• For example, consider the following:

How many minutes would it take Brenna to read 2r words if she reads at an average rate of 3s words per minute?

$$\text{(A) } \frac{2r}{3s} \quad \text{(B) } \frac{3s}{2r} \quad \text{(C) } 6rs \quad \text{(D) } \frac{40r}{s} \quad \text{(E) } \frac{s}{40r}$$

Answer. A. Although we solve this problem by assigning value to r and s, we can solve it more easily with a Rate Table. If Brenna reads 2r words at a **rate** of 3s words per minute, then we know:

R	×	T	=	W
3s	×	t	=	2r

• The correct answer is therefore (A), since it takes Brenda $\frac{2r}{3s}$ minutes to read 2r words:

$$3s \times t = 2r \quad \rightarrow \quad t = \frac{2r}{3s}$$

➢ However, if a problem seems CONFUSING or TRICKY in any way, we strongly encourage you to assign numbers instead.

• Remember, when assigning numbers, always choose numbers that are EASY to work with and that work well together.

• Likewise, do NOT pick the SAME number more than once, AVOID numbers you see in the question or the answer choices, and STAY AWAY from 0, 1, and 100.

➢ Finally, when plugging numbers into the answer choices, try answer choice (A) first. If (A) doesn't work, try (E) next.

• The correct answer to Asswhole problems is frequently (A) or (E), so trying (A) and then (E) may save you time.

- Consider the following:

Lydia buys a book of 200 identical stamps at a total cost of p dollars. If Lydia then sells each stamp at a rate that is 40 percent above the original, then, in terms of p, for how many dollars will each stamp be sold?

(A) $140\,p$ **(B)** $\dfrac{7p}{20}$ **(C)** $\dfrac{p}{200}+40$ **(D)** $\dfrac{140}{p}\times100$ **(E)** $\dfrac{7p}{1,000}$

Answer. E. While this problem can be solved algebraically, we can also solve it by assigning a value to p. To start, let's make $p = 400$.

> ➤ 400 is a good choice, **since it is not found in the question or the answer choices.** It also **produces whole numbers** when we use it, so it's easy to work with.

- Hence, if Lydia buys 200 stamps for \$400, she originally pays \$2 per stamp, as \$400/200 stamps = \$2/stamp.

- According to the problem, Lydia sells each stamp at a rate that is 40% percent above the original. If her stamps originally cost her \$2 each, she will sell each stamp for \$2.80, since 40% of \$2.00 = $4 \times 10\%$ = $4 \times \$0.20$ = \$0.80, and \$0.80 **above** \$2 = \$2.80. This is our TARGET answer.

> ➤ To finish the problem, we only have to **plug $p = 400$ into the answer choices to see which of them equals \$2.80**.

- Let's start with (A). (A) is not the correct answer since it does NOT equal 2.8:

$$(A)\ 140p \quad \longrightarrow \quad 140(400) = \boxed{56,000}$$

- Next, let's test (E). Since (E) equals 2.8, it is the correct answer.

$$(E)\ \frac{7p}{1,000} \quad \longrightarrow \quad \frac{7(400)}{1,000} = \frac{7(4)}{10} = \boxed{2.8}$$

- We could test out the remaining answer choices, but there's no need: we've already identified the correct answer.

Rare or Advanced Concepts

---

(9) Travelers & Trips – On rare occasions, GRE rate problems involve multiple travelers or multiple trips.

• For example, a question might involve a single traveler jogging from her house to her school and then walking back, or two trains racing towards one another.

    ➤ In many ways, Traveler & Trip problems are a lot like Working Together problems. To solve them, you first want to set up a RATE TABLE.

• At the top of the table place the rate formula: $R \times T = D$. Beneath it, place a row representing the rate, time, and work for EACH traveler or trip.

	R × T = D
Trip 1	
Trip 2	
Total	

• At the bottom of the table, place a TOTAL row in which rates, times, or distances may be ADDED or SUBTRACTED.

    ➤ However, Traveler & Trip problems differ from Working Together problems in a couple of key ways.

• For starters, Traveler & Trip problems often involve TRICKY relationships between the rates and times of the various parties. The ability to represent these relationships correctly is PIVOTAL to many problems.

• Here's a quick rundown of those relationships:

    1. **The party that travels LONGER or more SLOWLY has the GREATER time**, since it spends more time traveling.

• For example, if "Alex drives a certain distance 2/3 of an hour faster than Bill," Bill has the greater time because he spends more time driving. Thus, Bill's **time** $= t + 2/3$ and Alex's **time** $= t$. We could also let Bill $= t$ and Alex $= t - 2/3$, since Alex spends less time traveling.

2. **If two parties LEAVE at the same time and then MEET, they have the SAME time**, since both parties simultaneously start and stop traveling.

- Hence, if "Riley and Sophie both leave at 1 pm to meet at a local restaurant," Riley and Sophie travel for the same length of time upon meeting. Thus, we would let Riley's **time** = t and Sophie's **time** = t.

3. **The party that travels FASTER has the GREATER rate.** Likewise, the party that travels more slowly has the smaller rate.

- For instance, if "Callie walks twice as quickly as Darla," then Callie's rate should be double Darla's rate, since Callie is the faster walker. Thus, we would let Darla's **rate** = r and Callie's **rate** = $2r$.

  ➤ Traveler & Trip problems also differ from Working Together problems in that the details of the problem often CHANGE what happens in the TOTAL row.

- In general, every Traveler & Trip problem presents 1 of 4 scenarios, each of which implies something different about the relationships between the rates, times, and distances of the trips or travelers.

- We call these scenarios "the JOURNEY", "the CRASH", "SAME DISTANCE", and the "CHASE".

  ➤ JOURNEY PROBLEMS involve a single traveler (e.g. a car, jogger, train, boat, or cyclist) whose trip contains more than one stage.

- For example, a train may go from town A to town B at one rate, but from town B to town C at another. Or a cyclist may spend 1/3 of his or her ride traveling uphill, but the rest traveling downhill.

- To solve such problems, you must ADD the TIMES and DISTANCES of the various stages in the total row. You CANNOT, however, add the RATES.

  ➤ We add the times and distances because it is logical: the distance of any trip equals the sum of its various stages. The same is true of its time.

- **The rates, however, do not logically add.** If a cyclist rides uphill at a rate of 10 mph and 15 mph downhill, he or she does not average 25 mph for the entire ride.

- Let's look at a JOURNEY problem:

Janet took a two-day hike. On the second day she walked 3 hours longer and at an average rate 2 miles per hour faster than she did on the first day. If during those two days Janet walked a total of 48 miles and spent a total of 15 hours walking, how far did she walk, in miles, on the second day?

(A) 32   (B) 35   (C) 36   (D) 39   (E) 40

Answer. C. If Janet walked for a total of 15 hours, and did so for three more hours on day two than on day one, then she walked 9 hours on day two and 6 hours on day one.

➢ Likewise, if Janet's average rate on day two was 2 mph faster than on day one, then her rate for day two was $r + 2$ and her rate for day one r.

	R	×	T	=	D
Day 1	r	×	6	=	???
Day 2	$r + 2$	×	9	=	???
Total	???	×	15	=	48

According to our Distance Table, Janet walked a distance of $6r$ on day 1 and a distance of $9r + 18$ on day 2, since each row multiplies to a distance.

- If we fill enter this information into the table, we see that the two distances must ADD to 48 miles, since their combined distance logically equals the distance of the trip.

	R	×	T	=	D
Day 1	r	×	6	=	$6r$
Day 2	$r + 2$	×	9	=	$9r + 18$
Total	???	×	15	=	48

➢ Thus, we know that $r = 2$, since:

$$6r + (9r + 18) = 48$$
$$15r = 30$$
$$r = 2$$

- If Janet walked a distance of $9r + 18$ miles on day two, and $r = 2$, she therefore walked 36 miles that day, since $9(2) + 18 = 36$. Thus, the correct answer is (C).

➢ **CRASH PROBLEMS** involve two parties traveling DIRECTLY TOWARDS one another (as if they'll crash) or AWAY FROM one another (as if fleeing a crash site).

- For example, two trains may hurtle directly at one another, or two joggers may run away from the same school in opposite directions.

Chapter 5: Rates

- To solve such problems, simply remember that the individual DISTANCES must ADD to the distance that SEPARATES them. You can also ADD the RATES — if the two parties travel for the same length of time.

   ➤ Imagine two cars, 50 miles apart. If they travel directly towards one another, and car A travels 20 miles before they meet, then car B must have traveled the other 30.

- Thus, their combined distances add to 50 miles, a distance equal to the distance that initially separates them.

- Similarly, if from 1 p.m. to 3 p.m. Celeste jogs towards Dora at an average rate of 6 mph and Dora jogs towards Celeste at an average rate of 4 mph, then they travel 20 miles collectively, giving them an average rate of 10 mph for the two-hour period.

   ➤ However, you CANNOT add the TIMES. To understand why, imagine that Anna and Beth leave a restaurant in opposite directions, each driving at a rate of 30 mph.

- If both of them leave at 9 p.m. and return home at 10 p.m., they each spend 1 hour driving. If we were to add those times, however, we would be saying that it takes Anne and Beth 2 hours to return home.

- Obviously, this is false, since their trips start at 9 p.m. and end at 10 p.m.

   ➤ To ensure that you get a proper feel for CRASH problems, let's look at two examples.

- The first involves travelers moving directly towards one another, while the second involves travelers moving away from one another. Notice how the two problems are identical from a mathematical perspective, despite their logistic differences.

- Consider the following:

Trains A and B are 400 miles apart. At 11:00 a.m. train A begins to travel towards train B at a rate of 120 mph. At 11:30 a.m. train B begins to travel towards train A at a rate of 220 mph. At what time do the two trains meet?

(A) 12:15 p.m.   (B) 12:20 p.m.   (C) 12:30 p.m.   (D) 12:45 p.m.   (E) 1:00 p.m.

Answer. C. According to the problem, train A travels at a rate of 120 mph, train B travels at a rate of 220 mph, and the two trains are 400 miles apart.

- If train A leaves at 11:00 a.m. and train B at 11:30 a.m., then by the time they meet, **train A has traveled ½ an hour longer.** Thus, we can let B's time $= t$, and A's time $= t + ½$.

	R	×	T	=	D
A	120	×	$t + ½$	=	$120t + 60$
B	220	×	t	=	$220t$
Total				=	400

According to our Distance Table, train A travels a distance of $120t + 60$ and train B a distance of $220t$, since each row multiplies to a distance.

- Our table also shows that $120t + 60$ and $220t$ must add to a total of 400 miles, since **the distances of a crash problem always add to the distance that separates the traveling parties.** Thus, if $120t + 60 + 220t = 400$, then $t = 1$, since:

$$120t + 60 + 220t = 400 \;\rightarrow\; 340t = 340 \;\rightarrow\; t = 1$$

- Since train B begins moving at 11:30 a.m. and travels for a total of 1 hour before meeting train A, the two trains must meet at 12:30 p.m. Thus, the correct answer is (C).

At 1 p.m., Jim and Bill leave school, running in <u>opposite</u> directions. Jim runs at an average rate of 6 mph and Billy at an average rate of 4 mph. If Jim runs 20 minutes more than Billy, and they are 17 miles apart when both stop, how far did Billy run?

(A) 4 miles   (B) 4.5 miles   (C) 5 miles   (D) 5.5 miles   (E) 6 miles

Answer. E. According to the problem, Jim runs at a rate of 6 mph, Billy runs at a rate of 4 mph, and the two boys are 17 miles apart when they get home.

- If Jim runs 20 minutes **more** than Billy, then his time must be ⅓ **of an hour longer.** Thus, we can let Jim's time $= t + ⅓$ and Billy's time $= t$.

	R	×	T	=	D
Jim	6	×	$t + ⅓$	=	$6t + 2$
Billy	4	×	t	=	$4t$
Total					17

According to our Distance Table, Jim travels a distance of $6t + 2$ and Billy travels a distance of $4t$, since each row in the table multiplies to a distance.

- Our table also shows that $6t + 2$ and $4t$ must add to a total of 17 miles, since **the distances of a crash problem always add to the distance that separates the traveling parties.** Thus, if $6t + 2 + 4t = 17$, then $t = 1.5$, since:

$$6t + 2 + 4t = 17 \;\rightarrow\; 10t = 15 \;\rightarrow\; t = 1.5$$

- Therefore, Billy must have walked 6 miles, since he traveled $4t$ miles, and $4(1.5) = 6$. Thus, the correct answer is (E).

> ➢ [SAME DISTANCE] problems involve two trips of the same distance.

• Such problems are the most commonly encountered type of Traveler & Trip question, since there are a number of scenarios that imply trips of the same length. Typical setups include:

The <u>Roundtrip</u>: one party goes to, and returns from, the same location.
The <u>Copycat</u>: one traveler takes the same trip as another.
The <u>Hypothetical</u>: what would happen if an actual trip were taken at a different rate.

• It is not essential that you memorize every possible scenario that implies two trips of equal distance.

> ➢ What is important is that you recognize such scenarios when they occur, since the only way to solve SAME DISTANCE problems is to SET the distances EQUAL.

• In most cases, you should NOT add the rates, times, or distances. The only exception is the ROUNDTRIP. A roundtrip is essentially a journey in which each stage of the trip happens to have the same length and, as we've seen, the TIMES and DISTANCES of such problems should always be added.

• Let's look at a SAME DISTANCE problem:

Alice drove nonstop on a trip from her home to Phoenix. If her average speed for the trip had been 1.5 times as fast, the trip would have taken 4 hours. In hours, how long did it take Alice to drive to Phoenix?

(A) 2 (B) 3.2 (C) 4 (D) 5.6 (E) 6

Answer: E. This problem presents two scenarios: Alice's actual trip and what would have happened if she had traveled at a faster rate.

> ➢ According to the problem, if Alice were to have driven at a rate 1.5 times as fast as her actual rate, the trip would have taken her 4 hours.

• Since neither rate is known, we can let her **actual rate** = r and her **hypothetical rate = 1.5r.**

	R	×	T	=	D
Act	r	×	t	=	rt
Hypo	1.5r	×	4	=	$6r$
Total					

According to our Distance Table, Alice traveled a distance of rt when she drove to Phoenix, and would have traveled a distance of $6r$ had she driven 1.5 times as fast.

- Because her actual trip and her hypothetical trip both start from her home and end in Phoenix, the two distances are the same.

  ➢ Therefore, we can set them equal. Doing so proves that the correct answer is (E), since Alice's actual trip to Phoenix took t hours:

$$rt = 6r \rightarrow t = 6$$

- A second example for you:

Dwayne runs from his house to a river at an average rate of 12 miles per hour and then immediately walks back along the same route at an average rate of 4 miles per hour. If it takes Dwayne 30 minutes to get to the river and back, what is the distance, in miles, between Dwayne's house and the river?

(A) 0.8 (B) 1.2 (C) 1.5 (D) 1.8 (E) 2.1

Answer: C. Since Dwayne runs from his house to the river and returns along the same route, his journey is a **roundtrip**: each stage of his trip has the same distance.

  ➢ The problem states that Dwayne runs to the river at 12 mph, walks home at 4 mph, and takes half an hour to get to the river and back.

- Thus, if we let the time for his **run** = t, then the time for his **walk** = $\frac{1}{2} - t$, since the two times add to one half: $t + (\frac{1}{2} - t) = \frac{1}{2}$.

	R	×	T	=	D
Run	12	×	t	=	$12t$
Walk	4	×	$\frac{1}{2} - t$	=	$2 - 4t$
Total			$\frac{1}{2}$		

According to our Distance Table, Dwayne travels a distance of $12t$ going to the river and a distance of $2 - 4t$ returning, since each row in the table multiplies to a distance.

  ➢ Because the two distances are the **same**, we can set them equal to solve for t. Thus, $t = 1/8$, since:

$$12t = 2 - 4t \rightarrow 16t = 2 \rightarrow t = 2/16 = 1/8$$

- Therefore, Dwayne's house must be 1.5 miles from the river, since he ran $12t$ miles to get there, and $12t = 12 \times 1/8 = 12/8 = 1.5$ miles. Thus, the correct answer is (C).

Chapter 5: Rates

> ➢ **CHASE PROBLEMS** involve two parties traveling in the same direction but at different speeds.

• In most cases, one party catches up to another. For example, a faster runner might give a slower runner a head start, only to chase him or her down at the end of the run.

• Such problems are actually SAME DISTANCE problems, since the two parties start running at a common spot and stop at one, too. Like all Same Distance problems, you can solve them by setting the distances equal.

> ➢ Every now and then, however, the faster party either FAILS to catch up to the slower party or SURPASSES it upon catching up.

• To solve such problems, you need to treat the TIMES and DISTANCES as RELATIVE.

• Thus, if John is currently 2 miles behind Bill, but stops running 4 miles ahead, the <u>relative</u> difference between their **distances** is 6 miles. Likewise, if John runs at the rate of 10 mph and Bill at the rate of 8 mph, the <u>relative</u> difference in their **rates** is 2 mph. As such, it would take John 3 hours to get 4 miles ahead of Bill, since he starts 2 miles behind and gains 2 miles every hour that transpires.

> ➢ Usually, in such problems, you'll find that the two parties travel the SAME length of TIME. Be sure that you DON'T add those times.

• For instance, if Ally chases Brenda from 10 a.m. to 11 a.m., they each spend 1 hour traveling. If we were to add those times, however, we would be saying that Ally and Brenda chase one another for 2 hours, which is false: their trips start at 10 a.m. and end at 11 a.m.

• To get a better sense of how all this fits together, consider the following:

Cars A and B are moving east at constant rates. Car A is traveling at a rate of 60 miles per hour and car B at a rate of 50 miles per hour. If car A is currently 10 miles behind car B, how long will it take for car A to catch car B and pull 20 miles ahead?

(A) 2.75   (B) 3   (C) 3.25   (D) 3.5   (E) 3.75

Answer: B. Since the two cars **chase** one another throughout the problem, their respective times are identical. Thus, we can let both **times** = t.

• We can also let the **total time** = t, since the time elapsed over the course of the chase is identical to the time that car A spends chasing and surpassing car B (or that car B spends eluding and chasing car A).

> ➤ The **relative distance** that car A gains on car B is 30 miles, since it closes a gap of 10 miles before pulling ahead 20 miles.

• Thus, we can place a 30 in the "total distance" portion of our table. The **relative rate** at which car A gains on car B is 10 mph, since car A travels at 60 mph and car B at 50 mph. Thus, we can place a 10 in the "total rate" portion of our table.

	R	×	T	=	D
Car A	60	×	t	=	**60t**
Car B	50	×	t	=	**50t**
Total	**10**	×	t	=	**30**

Given this information, there are two ways we can solve the problem. The fastest way is to use the information in the TOTAL row of the table.

> ➤ Thus, since $10 \times t = 30$, we know that $t = 3$ hours. The correct answer is therefore (B). Alternatively, we can SUBTRACT the distances in the distance column, like so:

$$60t - 50t = 30 \;\rightarrow\; 10t = 30 \;\rightarrow\; t = 3$$

• We can subtract the rates and distances in a CHASE problem of this sort because the relationships are RELATIVE. When we say that car A is gaining 10 mph on car B, we're saying that the DIFFERENCE in the rates is 60 mph – 50 mph = 10 mph. Likewise, when we say that car A must gain 30 miles on car B, we're saying the distance traveled by car A minus the distance traveled by B equals 30 miles.

> ➤ The relationships within these scenarios have been SUMMARIZED below. If an entry has been left blank, it means "do nothing".

• Remember, the trips of a ROUNDTRIP have the same distance, but are also part of a journey. Thus, you can set their distances equal <u>OR</u> add their times and distances.

	RATES	TIMES	DISTANCES
JOURNEY		Add	Add
CRASH	Add*		Add
SAME DISTANCE			Set Equal
CHASE	Relative	Same	Relative

*only if the two parties travel for the <u>same</u> length of time

• Likewise, CHASE problems in which one party catches another are also SAME DISTANCE problems, so you can solve them by setting the distances equal.

(10) Altered Rates – Every now and then, a rate problem will involve a traveler or worker that speeds up, slows down, or stops.

- For instance, a cyclist may slow down while going up hill, a motorcycle may speed up after passing a car, or a machine may break down in the middle of a job.

  ➢ Although such problems can seem difficult, they are not much different from the problems we've already covered.

- To solve them, first calculate what happens BEFORE the change. Then then determine what happens AFTER it. To get a sense of how this works, consider the following:

Leah can complete job *J* on her own in 3 hours and Massey can complete the same job on her own in 5 hours. If Leah and Massey start working on job *J* together at 12:00 p.m., and Massey quits at 1:00 p.m., at what time will the job be completed?

(A) 1:48 p.m.   (B) 2:00 p.m.   (C) 2:12 p.m.   (D) 2:24 p.m.   (E) 2:30 p.m.

Answer: D. │ **Before Massey quits** │, Leah works at a rate of 1/3 job per hour and Massey works at a rate of 1/5 job per hour. Together, therefore, they work at a combined rate of 8/15 job per hour, as $1/5 + 1/3 = 8/15$.

	R	×	T	=	W
Leah	1/3	×	3	=	1
Massey	1/5	×	5	=	1
Together	**8/15**	×	**1**	=	**8/15**

Since Leah and Massey both start at 12:00 p.m., but Massey quits at 1:00 p.m., they work together for exactly **1 hour**. As our "Before" table shows, they will complete 8/15 of the job during this time, as 8/15 job per hr × 1 hr = 8/15 job.

│ **After Massey quits** │, only 7/15 of the job remains to be completed, since Leah and Massey have already done 8/15 of the job. However, Leah is now the ONLY person working, so this work will be done at Leah's rate of 1/3 of a job per hour.

	R	×	T	=	W
Leah	1/3	×	*t*	=	7/15

According to our "After" table, this work will be done in $1\frac{2}{5}$ hours, since:

$$t = \frac{7}{5\cancel{15}} \cdot \frac{\cancel{3}}{1} = \frac{7}{5} = 1\frac{2}{5}$$

- Since $1\frac{2}{5}$ hours equates to 1 hour and 24 minutes, and Massey quit at 1:00 p.m., Leah will finish the job at 2:24 p.m. Therefore, the correct answer is (D).

• Let's take a look at a second example, this time using travelers rather than workers:

Van A is currently 4 miles behind Van B. Vans A and B are traveling at constant rates of 62 mph and 58 mph, respectively. How long will it take, in hours, for Van A to pull 6 miles ahead of Van B, if Van A slows down to 60 mph once it catches up to Van B? Assume neither van stops at any point.

(A) 3   (B) 3.5   (C) 4   (D) 4.5   (E) 5

Answer: C. Since Van A and Van B are traveling in the same direction, but at different speeds, this is a CHASE problem.

	R	×	T	=	D
Van A	62	×	t	=	$62t$
Van B	58	×	t	=	$58t$
Total	4	×	t	=	4

Before Van A slows, Van A and Van B have a **relative rate** of 4 mph, since 62 mph – 58 mph = 4 mph. They also have a **relative distance** of 4 miles, since Van A is initially 4 miles behind Van B.

• Thus, it takes 1 hour for Van A to catch Van B, since the Total row and Distance Column of our "Before" table BOTH indicate that $4t = 4$.

After Van A slows, Van A and Van B have a **relative rate** of 2 mph, since Van B has a new rate of 60 mph, and 60 mph – 58 mph = 2 mph. They also have a **relative distance** of 6 miles, since Van A is to pull 6 miles ahead of Van B.

	R	×	T	=	D
Van A	60	×	t	=	$60t$
Van B	58	×	t	=	$58t$
Total	2	×	t	=	6

Thus, it will take 3 hours for Van A to pull 6 miles ahead of Van B, since the Total row and Distance column of our "After" table BOTH indicate that $2t = 6$.

• If it takes 1 hour for Van A to catch Van B and 3 hours to pull an additional 6 miles ahead, it will therefore take 4 hours for Van A to do both. Thus, the correct answer is (C).

(11) The Average Rate Trap – Every now and then, the GRE will test your knowledge of rates with a question like the following:

Train X traveled from city A to city B at a rate of 40 miles per hour and returned from city B to city A along the same route at a rate of 60 miles per hour.

Quantity A	Quantity B
The average rate of train X	48 mph

• If you're like most test-takers, your initial impression may be that Quantity A is larger than Quantity B, since the average of 40 and 60 is 50. Unfortunately, this is MISTAKEN.

➢ When a traveler makes two trips of the SAME DISTANCE, the traveler's average rate will ALWAYS be closer to the SLOWER of the rates.

• To understand why, imagine that Maria drives 60 miles at a rate of 60 mph, and then bikes back along the same path at 10 mph.

• The average rate for her trip could hardly be 35 mph, since she spends a LOT more time biking than driving.

➢ To determine an AVERAGE RATE, you need to know the TOTAL length of the trip and the TOTAL time that it took.

• If Maria drives at a rate of 60 mph and bikes at a rate of 10 mph, it takes her 1 hour to drive the 60 miles but 6 hours to walk it.

• Thus, her average rate for the trip is roughly 17 mph, since the total distance of her trip is 120 miles and the total time to make it is 7 hours.

➢ In most Average Rate problems, you will NOT be given a DISTANCE.

• In such cases, you can PICK a DISTANCE. Although you can pick ANY length that you want, we encourage you pick a distance that is EASY to work with.

• For example, given rates of 30 mph and 45 mph, you ought to pick a distance of 90 miles, since 90 is clearly divisible by both 30 and 45. Likewise, given rates of 24 mph and 36 mph, you should pick a distance of 72 miles, as 72 is clearly divisible by both 24 and 36.

- Let's return to the problem we saw at the start of this section:

Train X traveled from city A to city B at a rate of 40 miles per hour and returned from city B to city A along the same route at a rate of 60 miles per hour.

<u>Quantity A</u>	<u>Quantity B</u>
The average rate of train X	48 mph

Answer: C. As discussed, Quantity A cannot equal 50 mph, since a traveler's average rate will always be **closer** to the **slower** of his or her rates.

  ➤ To solve an Average Rate problem, we need to know the traveler's **total** distance and **total time**.

- Here, each stage of train X's trip has the **same distance, but no particular lengths were given.** Thus, we can pick a distance.

	R	×	T	=	D
To A	40	×	3	=	<u>120</u>
To B	60	×	2	=	<u>120</u>
Total	r	×	5	=	<u>240</u>

Since the given rates are 40 mph and 60 mph, let's make the distance between the cities 120 miles, as 120 is easily divisible by both 40 and 60.

- According to our Distance Table, train X traveled a total distance of 240 miles and took a total time of 5 hours to do so, since it takes 3 hours to travel 120 miles at 40 mph and 2 hours to travel 120 miles at 60 mph.

  ➤ The **total row** of the table contains the equation $r \times 5 = 240$, so the average rate of the trip must have been 48 mph, as:

$$r = \frac{240}{5} = \frac{480}{10} = 48$$

Double your numbers to divide by 10 instead of 5!

- Thus, the correct answer is (C), since the two quantities are equal.

(12) Exponential Growth – Exponential Growth problems are very similar to the Linear Growth problems we discussed in Algebraic Word Problems.

• The two forms of growth are similar in that each occurs at regular intervals. They differ, however, in that **Exponential Growth occurs at identical FACTORS** rather than identical increments.

➤ To understand the difference, imagine a population of insects that triples in size every month.

• If the population were to start at 200, it would grow to 600 by the end of the 1st month, to 1,800 by the end of the 2nd month, and to 5,400 by the end of the 3rd month.

• In other words, even though the population is increasing in the same manner each month (i.e. tripling), the increments CHANGE. Thus, from the 1st month to the 2nd the population increases by 1,200, but from the 2nd month to the 3rd it increases by 3,600.

➤ As with Linear Growth problems, the easiest way to start an Exponential Growth problem is with a t-chart.

• In the left column, place the intervals at which the growth occurs. In the right column, place any sizes you know. Then, label the unknown growth x.

• For every interval you "jump" down the t-chart, MULTIPLY the size by x.

➤ For example, imagine a population of bacteria that grows by some fixed factor **every 2 hours**, and **whose size is 6,000 at 12 p.m. and 54,000 at 4 p.m.**

• We could represent that information as follows:

	HOUR	SIZE	
The growth happens	12 p.m.	6,000	x for ONE "jump"
every 2 hours, so the	2 p.m.	$6,000 \cdot x$	from 12 p.m. x^3 for
INTERVALS are 2 hours	4 p.m.	$6,000 \cdot x^2$	THREE "jumps"
apart.	6 p.m.	$6,000 \cdot x^3$	from 12 p.m.

• **As our chart shows**, the size of the population at 4 p.m. is $6,000 \cdot x^2$, since 4 p.m. is TWO "jumps" down the t-chart. **According to the statement above**, however, the population at 4 p.m. is 54,000. Thus, we know that $6,000 \cdot x^2 = 54,000$.

- Given this equation, we can determine that $x = 3$, like so:

$$54,000 = 6,000 \cdot x^2 \quad \rightarrow \quad \frac{54,000}{6,000} = 9 = x^2 \quad \rightarrow \quad x = \pm 3$$

> Since $x = $ **the rate of growth**, we know that the population triples every 2 hours. (Note, btw, that -3 is NOT a solution since growth rates cannot be negative.)

- Thus, if we need to determine the size of the population at 2 p.m. or 4 p.m., we simply need to plug $x = 3$ back into the chart. For example, the size of the population at 2 p.m. is given as $6,000 \cdot x$, so we know the population at the time equals $6,000 \cdot 3 = 18,000$.

- To give you get a better feel for solving Exponential Growth problems, let's work through a practice example together:

By some fixed factor, a colony of ants increases in size every three months. If 9 months from now the size of the colony will be 81,000, and 3 months ago it was 1,000, how large is the colony currently?

(A) 3×10^2 (B) 5×10^2 (C) 10^3 (D) 1.5×10^3 (E) 3×10^3

Answer. E. Since the size of colony increases by a fixed factor, its growth is exponential. To determine that rate, we can set up the following t-chart:

	MONTH	SIZE	
The growth happens every 3 months, so the INTERVALS are 3 months apart.	3 mo. ago	1,000	x for ONE "jump"
	now	$1,000 \cdot x$	down the chart. x^3 for
	3 mo.	$1,000 \cdot x^2$	THREE "jumps" down
	6 mo.	$1,000 \cdot x^3$	the chart.
	9 mo.	$1,000 \cdot x^4$	

> As our chart shows, 3 months ago the size of the population was 1,000, so 9 months from now it will be $1,000 \cdot x^4$, since 9 months is FOUR "jumps" down the chart.

- **According to the problem**, however, 9 months from now the size of the colony will be 81,000. Thus, we know that $1,000 \cdot x^4 = 81,000$. We can use this equation to solve for x:

$$81,000 = 1,000 \cdot x^4 \quad \rightarrow \quad \frac{81,000}{1,000} = 81 = x^4 \quad \rightarrow \quad x = \pm 3$$

- Since $x = $ **the rate of growth**, we know that the population triples in size every 3 months. According to our chart, the size of the population is **currently** $1,000 \cdot x$. If $x = 3$, then that population must equal $1,000 \cdot 3 = 3,000$, or 3×10^3. Thus, the correct answer is (E).

Practice Questions

(13) Problem Sets – The following questions have been arranged into three groups: fundamental, intermediate, and rare or advanced.

• Whether you're aiming for a perfect score or a score closer to average, mastery of the concepts in the FUNDAMENTAL questions is absolutely essential.

  ➤ As you might expect, the INTERMEDIATE questions are more difficult but are essential for test-takers who need an above-average score or higher.

• Finally, the RARE or ADVANCED questions test concepts that are very sophisticated or seldom encountered on the GRE. Mastery of such questions is required only if you need a math score above the 90th percentile.

• As always, if you find yourself confused, bogged down with busy work, or stuck, don't be afraid to fall back on your "Plan B" strategies!

Fundamental

On a recent trip, Lenore drove 120 miles in 4 hours using gasoline that cost her $3.49 per gallon.

Quantity A	Quantity B
1.	
Lenore's average rate for the trip in miles per hour	Lenore's gas mileage for the trip in miles per gallon

2.   When walking, a certain person takes 24 complete steps in 15 seconds. At this rate, how many steps does this person take in 48 seconds?

Round your answer to the nearest <u>whole number</u>.

[   ]

Quantity A	Quantity B
3.	
The time required to travel x miles at y miles per hour	The time required to travel $\frac{x}{4}$ miles at $4y$ miles per hour

Cyclist A traveled 3/5 kilometers and Cyclist B traveled 60,000 centimeters.

| Quantity A | Quantity B |

4. The distance that A traveled   The distance that B traveled

5. A car got 28 miles per gallon using gasoline that cost $3.15 per gallon. What was the approximate cost, in dollars, of the gasoline used in driving the car 310 miles?

    (A) $15 (B) $22 (C) $35 (D) $45 (E) $55

Working at constant rates, machine A completely builds n chairs in 0.5 hours and machine B completely builds n chairs in 0.8 hours, where n is a positive integer.

| Quantity A | Quantity B |

6. The number of chairs completely   The number of chairs completely
    built by A in 6 hours   built by B in 9 hours

Country	Value of 1 United States Dollar
Switzerland	0.92 franc
India	44.45 rupee

| Quantity A | Quantity B |

7. The dollar value of 1 Indian rupee   The dollar value of 1 Swiss franc
    according to the table above   according to the table above

8. Point P lies on the exterior of wheel W. If point P is 40 centimeters from the center of wheel W, what is the distance traveled, in centimeters, by point P in 20 seconds if wheel W rotates at the rate of 180 revolutions per minute?

    (A) $1,600\pi$ (B) $2,400\pi$ (C) $3,200\pi$ (D) $4,800\pi$ (E) $6,400\pi$

9. How many minutes does it take to travel 180 miles at a rate of 400 miles per hour?

    ┌──────────┐
    │   │
    └──────────┘

n issues of journal N cost a total of $24.

Quantity A	Quantity B

10. The total cost, in dollars, of x issues of journal N $\dfrac{24x}{n}$

11. Machines A and B, working independently at constant rates, can do a certain job in 3 hours and in 4 hours, respectively. How long, in hours, would it take both machines, working together at their respective constant rates, to do 2/3 of the job?

(A) $\dfrac{6}{7}$ (B) $1\dfrac{1}{7}$ (C) $1\dfrac{2}{3}$ (D) $2\dfrac{3}{4}$ (E) $4\dfrac{2}{3}$

12. If train T travels at the rate of k kilometers per h hours, how many kilometers does train T travel in m minutes?

(A) $\dfrac{hk}{m}$ (B) $\dfrac{hm}{k}$ (C) $\dfrac{60hm}{k}$ (D) $\dfrac{60km}{h}$ (E) $\dfrac{km}{60h}$

Intermediate

13. Working at the same constant rate, 6 machines can produce 150 bolts in 20 seconds. At this same rate, how many bolts will 8 such machines produce in 3 minutes?

(A) 300   (B) 600   (C) 900   (D) 1,800   (E) 2,700

A store sells cups at the same price, regardless of the number of cups sold. n of these cups have a total price of p cents, and k of these cups have a total price of d cents.

Quantity A	Quantity B

14. dn kp

15. Working at a constant rate, machine A takes 2/3 of an hour to fill a certain tank to 1/5 of its capacity. How much more time will it take machine A to finish filling the tank?

(A) 1 hr 40 min   (B) 2 hr 10 min   (C) 2 hr 25 min   (D) 2 hr 40 min   (E) 3 hr 15 min

16. A rectangular floor measuring 6 yards by 5 yards is to be carpeted completely at a cost of n dollars per square foot. In terms of n, how many dollars will the carpeting cost? (1 yard = 3 feet)

    (A) $30n$ (B) $65n$ (C) $90n$ (D) $180n$ (E) $270n$

Working at the same constant rate, 5 machines can complete a certain task in 16 hours. 8 such machines can complete the same task in x hours.

Quantity A	Quantity B

17. x 12

18. How many revolutions will a windmill make in n minutes, at a rate of 240 revolutions per hour?

    (A) $240n$ (B) $4n$ (C) $\frac{4}{n}$ (D) $\frac{240}{n}$ (E) $\frac{14,400}{n}$

Quantity A	Quantity B

19.   The number of seconds   The number of minutes
         in s weeks   in $60s$ weeks

20. Working alone at their respective constant rates, machine R produces w widgets in 20 minutes and machine S produces w widgets in 30 minutes. How many minutes does it take machines R and S, working simultaneously and together at their respective constant rates, to produce $5w$ widgets?

21. A cyclist travels x miles in w hours and z minutes. What is the cyclist's speed in miles per hour?

    (A) $\frac{x}{w + 60z}$ (B) $\frac{60w + z}{x}$ (C) $\frac{60x}{w + z}$ (D) $\frac{w + z}{x}$ (E) $\frac{60x}{60w + z}$

22. In a certain country, a child is born every 4 seconds and a person dies every 7 seconds. Thus, the birth and death rates account for a population growth of one person every

    (A) $1\frac{3}{7}$ sec   (B) 3 sec   (C) $4\frac{2}{3}$ sec   (D) $9\frac{1}{3}$ sec   (E) 11 sec

23. Gasoline started leaking from a fuel tank yesterday at a constant rate of 0.002 gallons per second and continued leaking at this rate for 1 hour until the tank was 1/5 full. If the tank had been 4/5 full before the leaking began, then which of the following amounts exceed the capacity of the tank, in gallons?

    Indicate <u>all</u> such amounts.

    $\boxed{A}$ 10.4 $\boxed{B}$ 11.2 $\boxed{C}$ 12.1 $\boxed{D}$ 13.5 $\boxed{E}$ 14.0

24. The age of the moon is approximately 1.4×10^{17} seconds. Which of the following is nearest to the age of the moon, in years? (1 year is approximately 3.2×10^7 seconds.)

    (A) 4.4×10^9 (B) 5.9×10^9 (C) 6.7×10^9 (D) 1.5×10^{11} (E) 3.4×10^{11}

25. Water flows into an empty 480-gallon tank through pipe A and out of the tank through pipe B. If the rate of flow through pipe A is 2 gallons per second, how many gallons per second must flow through pipe B so that the tank is full in exactly 12 <u>minutes</u>?

    (A) $\frac{3}{8}$ (B) $\frac{1}{2}$ (C) $\frac{2}{3}$ (D) $\frac{4}{3}$ (E) $\frac{8}{3}$

$\boxed{\text{Rare or Advanced}}$

On a recent trip from her home to the beach, Nancy traveled in a direct path at a constant rate of 24 miles per hour. On her way home, she returned along the same path at a constant rate of 36 miles per hour.

Quantity A	Quantity B
The average rate, in miles per hour, of Nancy's trip	30

26.

27. Isaiah traveled 10 miles from his house to a store at an average speed of 50 miles per hour and returned home along the same route. What was Isaiah's average speed on his return home if the travel time for the two trips was 20 minutes, combined?

(A) 55 mph   (B) 60 mph   (C) 65 mph   (D) 70 mph   (E) 75 mph

David ran a certain distance in 2 hours. Bob ran that same distance, along the same route, in 3 hours, doing so at a speed 2 miles per hour slower than David.

Quantity A	Quantity B
28. The distance, in miles, that David ran	9.5

29. Tubes A and B independently drip water into a beaker at constant rates. If tubes A and B, working together, drip water four times as fast as tube A, and tube B takes 6 minutes to fill 1/2 the beaker, how long, in minutes, would it take tube A to fill 2/3 of the beaker if it were to work alone?

(A) 12   (B) 18   (C) 24   (D) 36   (E) 72

Cars S and T are 85 miles apart when car S begins to travel in the exact direction of car T at a constant rate of 60 miles per hour. Half an hour later, car T begins to travel at a rate of 80 miles per hour in the exact direction of car S.

Quantity A	Quantity B
30. The distance, in miles, that car S has traveled when the two cars cross paths	55

31. At 9:00 a.m., Bus A left a bus terminal and two hours later Bus B left the same terminal along the same route. If Bus A averaged 60 kilometers per hour and Bus B averaged 75 kilometers per hour until B passed A, at what time did B pass A?

(A) 2:00 p.m.   (B) 5:00 p.m.   (C) 6:00 p.m.   (D) 7:00 p.m.   (E) 9:00 p.m.

32. By some fixed factor, a population of worms increases in size every six months. If 1 year from now the size of the population will be 75,000, and 6 months ago it was 600, how large will the population be 6 months from now?

(A) 3×10^2 (B) 0.5×10^3 (C) 10^4 (D) 1.5×10^4 (E) 2.5×10^5

A motorcycle traveling at a certain constant speed takes 2 seconds longer to travel 1 mile than it would to travel 1 mile at 75 miles per hour.

	Quantity A	Quantity B
33.	The rate, in miles per hour, that the motorcycle is traveling	72

34. A certain thrift shop charges the same price for each umbrella that it sells. If the current price of each umbrella were to be increased by two dollars, four fewer of the umbrellas could be bought for one hundred and sixty dollars, excluding sales tax. What is the current price, in dollars, of each umbrella?

(A) 2   (B) 4   (C) 8   (D) 10   (E) 16

35. Fred walked 100 yards to his friend Gary's house at a rate of x yards per minute. If Fred had walked 10 yards per minute faster, he would have reached Gary's house in 5/6 of the time that it actually took.

	Quantity A	Quantity B
	The time, in minutes, that it took Fred to walk to Gary's house	2.5 minutes

36. Working independently at constant rates, pumps A and B can produce 1 gallon of water every $4p$ minutes and $4/p$ minutes, respectively. If pump A runs alone for q minutes and is later joined by pump B until 40 gallons of water are produced, for how many minutes will the two pumps run at the same time?

(A) $\dfrac{400p}{q}$ (B) $\dfrac{240+q}{p^2}$ (C) $\dfrac{200+q}{10p}$ (D) $\dfrac{600p}{120-q}$ (E) $\dfrac{160p-q}{1+p^2}$

37. On a recent commute, Helen traveled $2p$ percent of the entire distance at an average rate of 24 miles per hour. If Helen traveled the rest of the distance at an average rate of 40 miles per hour, what was her average rate, in terms of p, for the entire trip?

(A) $\dfrac{3,000}{p+75}$ (B) $\dfrac{p+40}{24}$ (C) $\dfrac{300+4p}{5}$ (D) $\dfrac{600}{120-p}$ (E) $\dfrac{4,000-p}{240}$

(14) Solutions – Video solutions for each of the previous questions can be found on our website at **www.sherpaprep.com/videos**.

- BOOKMARK this address for future visits!

    ➤ To view the videos, you'll need the LOGIN and PASSWORD that you created upon registering your copy of Word Problems.

- If you have yet to register your book yet, please go to **www.sherpaprep.com/activate** and enter your email address, last name, and shipping address.

- Be sure to provide the SAME last name and shipping address that you used to purchase your copy of Master Key to the GRE or to enroll in your GRE course with Sherpa Prep!

    ➤ When checking your answers, we encourage you to watch the solution for any problem that you answered INCORRECTLY

- The same goes for any problem that took you MORE than TWO MINUTES to solve.

- After digesting the explanation, REVISIT your mistake a couple of days later to ensure that the problem no longer poses issues to you.

    ➤ If you struggle to solve the problem a SECOND time, add it to your "LOG of ERRORS" and redo it every few weeks.

- Solving tricky questions MORE THAN ONCE is the best way to learn from your mistakes and to avoid similar difficulties on your actual exam.

Fundamental		Intermediate		Rare or Advanced	
1. D	11. B	13. D	23. C, D, E	26. B	36. E
2. 77	12. E	14. C	24. A	27. E	37. A
3. A		15. D	25. D	28. A	
4. C		16. E		29. C	
5. C		17. B		30. B	
6. A		18. B		31. D	
7. B		19. C		32. D	
8. D		20. 60		33. C	
9. 27		21. E		34. C	
10. C		22. D		35. B	

Chapter 6

Overlapping Sets

Overlapping Sets

To be discussed:

Fundamental Concepts

Whether you're aiming for a perfect score or a score closer to average, mastery of the following concepts is essential.

1   Introduction
2   The Overlapping Sets Table
3   Labeling Tables
4   PUQ's and FUQ's
5   Venn Diagrams
6   The Overlapping Sets Formula

Rare or Advanced Concepts

The following concepts are either advanced or are tested only on rare occasions. If you don't need an elite math score, don't waste your time!

7   Algebraic Relationships
8   Hidden Information
9   Maximization Problems
10 3-Part Overlapping Sets
11 Intersections & Unions

Practice Questions

There's no substitute for elbow grease. Practice your new skills to ensure that you internalize what you've studied.

12 Problem Sets
13 Solutions

Fundamental Concepts

(1) Introduction – Problems that involve the intersection of two or more groups are commonly known as Overlapping Sets problems.

• Overlapping Sets problems are somewhat rare for the GRE. In fact, most exams only contain a single example, if any.

> ➢ Some Data Interpretation questions, however, involve Overlapping Sets, so it's always possible that as many as 3 of your 40 exam questions test this topic.

• To get a sense of what an Overlapping Sets problem looks like, consider the following:

Washington High School has 100 students. 70 students study Spanish and 60 students study French. If 10 students study neither language and 40 study both, how many students only study French?

• In general, there are three ways to solve such problems:

1. With a Venn Diagram
2. With the Overlapping Sets Formula
3. With an Overlapping Sets Table

• Of the three, the Overlapping Sets Formula is generally the fastest strategy, but also the most limited. It is only helpful in certain situations. Venn diagrams are the most commonly taught strategy, but are not very effective for more difficult problems.

> ➢ Although all three strategies will be explained here, we strongly encourage you to master the Overlapping Sets Table.

• It is smart, fast, and effective, and works for easy and hard problems alike.

• That said, if you are more comfortable with Venn diagrams, feel free to stay with that strategy. Just be sure that you understand the table approach, too. It never hurts to know more than one strategy.

(2) The Overlapping Sets Table – To give you a sense of how the "Table" strategy works, let's take another look at the problem about Washington High School.

Washington High School has 100 students. 70 students study Spanish and 60 students study French. If 10 students study neither language and 40 study both, how many students only study French?

• This problem contains TWO general groups of students: those who study Spanish and those who study French. Because some of the students who study Spanish also study French, the two groups OVERLAP.

➢ Whenever two groups overlap, every member can always be categorized as either:

    1. In the FIRST group or NOT in the FIRST group
    2. In the SECOND group or NOT in the SECOND group

• For example, every student at Washington High School either studies Spanish or does not, studies French or does not. As such, a table can be drawn whose rows and columns correspond to these categories.

• Note that our Overlapping Sets Table also contains a **total row** and **total column**, giving it a total of NINE slots:

These students study BOTH French and Spanish	These students ONLY study French	ALL of the students who study French

	Spanish	No Spanish	Total
French	40		60
No French		10	
Total	70		100

ALL of the students who study Spanish	These students study NEITHER language	ALL of the students at the school

➢ As you can see, each slot in an Overlapping Sets Table represents a distinct group.

• For example, the **upper-left** slot represents the intersection of the "Spanish" and "French" categories, and thus indicates the number of students who study **both** languages. Likewise, the **center** slot represents the intersection of the "No Spanish" and "No French" categories, and thus indicates those students who study **neither** language.

➤ Once the data supplied by an Overlapping Sets problem has been inserted into the table, the problem can be solved by ADDING each row and column to its TOTAL.

• For example, our table about Washington High School can be completed as follows:

30 students ONLY study Spanish,
since 40 + 30 = 70

20 students ONLY study French,
since 40 + 20 = 60

	Spanish	No Spanish	Total
French	40	20	60
No French	30	10	40
Total	70	30	100

30 students do NOT study Spanish,
since 70 + 30 = 100

40 students do NOT study French,
since 60 + 40 = 100

• Thus, 20 students at Washington High School only study French, since the **upper-center** slot of our table represents the intersection of the "French" and "No Spanish" categories, and thus indicates the students who **only study French**.

➤ When solving Overlapping Sets problems, it's not always necessary to complete the entire table. In fact, some problems may not give you enough information to do so.

• You only need to complete the slot in question. Still, it can be USEFUL to complete the entire table, even if you don't need to. Doing so can **expose careless mistakes** that you might otherwise miss.

• For example, you might insert information into the wrong slot or incorrectly add critical numbers. Completing the table can reveal these mistakes, since certain portions of your table may not add up.

➤ It can also be helpful to CIRCLE the slot you need to solve for. Doing so will ensure that you determine the right information.

• For example, in the question about Washington High School, we needed to determine how many students only studied French. Thus, we could have circled the intersection of the "French" and "No Spanish" categories to remind ourselves what we needed to identify:

	Spanish	No Spanish	Total
French	40		60
No French		10	
Total	70		100

't a better feel for using the Overlapping Sets Table, consider the following:

We Beat Dogs Kennel has a total of 80 dogs. If 72 dogs are sad, 40 dogs are small, and 6 dogs are small and not sad, how many dogs are not small and sad?

(A) 35   (B) 36   (C) 37   (D) 38   (E) 39

Answer. D. "We Beat Dogs Kennel" has two groups of dogs: **those that are sad** and **those that are small**. Thus, every dog in the kennel is either sad or not sad, is small or not small.

According to the problem, the kennel has a **total** of 80 dogs, of which 72 **are sad**, 40 **are small**, and 6 **are small and not sad**. This information can be plugged into an Overlapping Set Table in the manner shown to the right.

	Sad	Not Sad	Total
Small		6	40
Not Small			
Total	72		80

	Sad	Not Sad	Total
Small	34	6	40
Not Small			
Total	72	8	80

As shown to the left, the **top and bottom rows** of this table can be completed with a 34 and an 8, respectively, since $\boxed{34}$ + 6 = 40 and 72 + $\boxed{8}$ = 80.

The remainder of the table can be completed in the manner shown to the right. As can be seen, 38 of the dogs at the kennel are not small and sad, since the **middle-left** slot of our table represents the intersection of the "Not Small" and "Sad" categories.

	Sad	Not Sad	Total
Small	34	6	40
Not Small	38	2	40
Total	72	8	80

(3) Labeling Tables – When building an Overlapping Sets Table, the "headline row" atop your table should reflect an "EITHER/OR" decision.

• The same is true of the "headline column" on the left edge. Remember, when two groups overlap, every member can be categorized as either:

   1. In the FIRST group or NOT in the FIRST group
   2. In the SECOND group or NOT in the SECOND group

• Your headline row and column must reflect these dichotomies. If either reads "In first/In second", or "Not in first/Not in second", you've **mislabeled** your table. Consider the following:

In a recent election, 40% of the participants voted "yes" to measure _A_, 60% voted "yes" to measure _B_, and 30% voted "no" to both measures. If 300 people voted, and everyone voted on each measure, how many participants voted "yes" to measure _A_?

• This problem has two groups of people: those who voted for measure _A_ and those who voted for measure _B_. The two groups overlap since some people voted for both measures.

   ➤ However, every participant made a choice: he or she voted for measure _A_, or didn't. The same is true for measure _B_.

• The following table would be a mistake, since the headline row does NOT reflect an "EITHER/OR" decision. The same is true of the headline column:

MISTAKE

	_A_	_B_	Total
No _A_			
No _B_			
Total			

• To set up a table correctly, our headline row and column must both reflect an "EITHER/OR" decision. Thus, a table for this problem should look like this:

CORRECT

	_A_	No _A_	Total
_B_			180
No _B_		90	
Total	120		300

(4) PUQ's and FUQ's – In our book titled <u>Arithmetic & "Plan B" Strategies</u>, we introduced two problems types that we like to call "PUQ's" and "FUQ's".

• As you may recall, the term "PUQ" is an acronym for "Percents with Unspecified Quantities". Similarly, the term "FUQ" stands for "Fractions with Unspecified Quantities".

➤ In those discussions, we suggested that the key to solving such problems is <u>to PICK NUMBERS</u>.

• Specifically, we recommended that you **pick 100** to solve PUQ's and that you **pick the product of the denominators** to solve FUQ's.

• Overlapping set problems occasionally surface as PUQ's or FUQ's. To solve such problems, simply let the number you choose be the total. Consider the following:

$\frac{1}{2}$ of the students in a class of boys are girls are boys. $\frac{1}{3}$ of the students in that class were absent on Tuesday and $\frac{1}{4}$ of those present were boys.

Quantity A	**Quantity B**
The number of girls that were absent on Tuesday	**1**

Answer: B. The class has two groups of people: **those who are boys** and **those who are absent**. Thus, every student in the class is either (1) a boy or a girl, (2) absent or present.

	Boys	Girls	Total
Absent			8
Present	4		16
Total	12	12	24

Because this problem has fractions but NO numbers, let's set the total equal to 24, which is the product of the problem's denominators.

The problem states that "1/2 of the students are boys" and that "1/3 of the students were absent". From this, we know that 12 of the students **are boys** and that 8 of the students **were absent**, since 1/2 of 24 = 12 and 1/3 of 24 = 8.

The problem also states that "1/4 of those present were boys". Thus, there must have been 4 **boys present**, since there were 16 students present, and 1/4 of 16 = 4.

Completing our table proves that zero **girls were absent** on Tuesday. As such, Quantity B is larger than Quantity A.

	Boys	Girls	Total
Absent	8	0	8
Present	4	12	16
Total	12	12	24

➢ But remember: if your question involves REAL numbers, you CAN'T pick numbers.

- PUQ's and FUQ's never contain real numbers. If you pick numbers for a problem with real numbers, you will likely contradict the information given in the problem.

- Consider the following:

In a certain class, 60 percent of the students wear glasses and 15 percent have brown hair but do not wear glasses. If the class has 8 students who do not wear glasses, what percentage of the class does not wear glasses and does not have brown hair?

(A) 10%   (B) 15%   (C) 20%   (D) 25%   (E) 30%

Answer: D. The class has two groups of students: **those who wear glasses** and **those who have brown hair**. Therefore, every student in the class either (1) wears glasses or does not wear glasses, (2) has brown hair or does not have brown hair.

	Glasses	No Glas.	Total
Brown		0.15x	
No Brown			
Total	0.6x	8	x

This problem states that 8 students **do not wear glasses**, so we CANNOT let the total number of students = 100. Instead, we must let the number of students = x, since it is unknown.

As such, if "60 percent of the students wear glasses", we can let the **total glasses group** = $0.6x$. Likewise, if "15 percent of the students have brown hair but do not wear glasses", we can let the **brown hair and no glasses group** = $0.15x$.

As can be seen from the table above, $0.6x + 8 = x$, proving that $x = 20$:

$$0.6x + 8 = x$$
$$8 = 0.4x \qquad \text{Subtract } 0.6x \text{ from both sides.}$$
$$\frac{8}{0.4} = \frac{80}{4} = 20 = x \qquad \text{Divide both sides by 0.4.}$$

If $x = 20$, the $0.15x = 0.15(20) = 3$. Plugging this information back into the matrix reveals that 5 students do not wear glasses or have brown hair.

	Glasses	No Glas.	Total
Brown		0.15x = 3	
No Brown		5	
Total	0.6x	8	20

Thus, 25% of the class does not wear glasses or have brown hair, since 5 of the 20 students in the class have no glasses and no brown hair.

(5) Venn Diagrams – As mentioned, problems involving Overlapping Sets can also be solved with Venn Diagrams.

• In fact, Venn Diagrams are the traditional manner in which most students are taught to solve such problems.

➤ Although Venn Diagrams offer a handy way to visualize the intersection of groups, we do NOT encourage you to use them to solve Overlapping Set problems.

• **Venn Diagrams are awkward to use and offer no real advantages to** the Overlapping Sets Table. This is particularly true of problems involving the intersection of two groups.

• Additionally, there is a more effective way of solving problems involving the intersection of three groups, too. You will find our discussion of them in our pool of Rare or Advanced topics, since such problems are quite rare for the GRE.

➤ This said, exam-makers occasionally design problems involving Venn Diagrams, so it is important that you understand how they work.

• The core concept is fairly simple: **each group is represented by a circle**. The overlap between the two circles represents the members in both groups. Everything outside the circles represents the members in neither group.

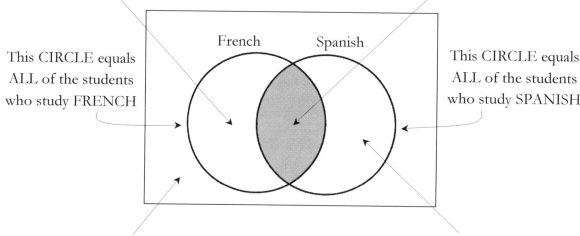

This SECTOR represents the students who ONLY study FRENCH

The OVERLAP represents the students who study BOTH languages

This CIRCLE equals ALL of the students who study FRENCH

This CIRCLE equals ALL of the students who study SPANISH

These students are OUTSIDE the circles and thus study NEITHER language

This SECTOR represents the students who ONLY study SPANISH

➢ Three-set diagrams share the same principles. As with two-set diagrams, each group is represented by a circle.

• The overlap between all three circles represents the members in ALL three groups. The overlap between TWO circles represents the members in both groups, but not the third. Everything outside the circles represents the members in none of the three groups.

This CIRCLE represents
the students who study FRENCH

These students study
ALL THREE languages

These students study
FRENCH and
SPANISH, but not
German

These students study
FRENCH and
GERMAN, but not
Spanish

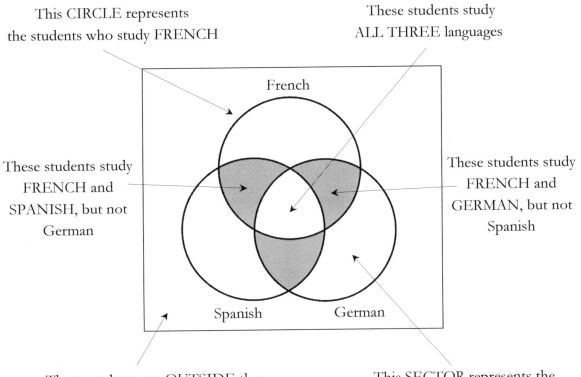

These students are OUTSIDE the
circles and thus study NONE of the languages

This SECTOR represents the
students who ONLY study GERMAN

➢ Remember, you only need to know how to interpret Venn Diagrams. You don't need to use them to solve problems.

• To get a sense of how the GRE might test your knowledge of Venn Diagrams, consider the following:

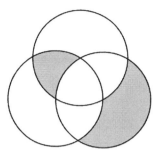

The area of each of the three circular regions in the figure above is 70, and the area of the intersection of exactly two circular regions is 25.

Quantity A	Quantity B
The sum of the areas of the shaded regions	50

Answer: B. According to the problem, the area of the intersection of exactly two circular regions is 25. The problem also states that each circle has a total area of 70:

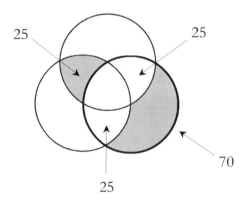

Since the circle highlighted in bold has an area of 70, and there are three intersections of exactly two circular regions — each with an area of 25 — WITHIN this diagram, **the shaded portion of the bold circle must have an area of 20 or less**, since:

$$70 - 25 - 25 = 20$$

Of course, **we don't know the area of the overlap of all three circles,** but it is irrelevant to the question. If the shaded portion of the bolded circle has an area of 20 or less, and the shaded region outside the bolded circle has an area of 25, then the sum of the areas of the two shaded regions cannot exceed 45, since $20 + 25 = 45$.

Thus, Quantity B must be larger than Quantity A.

(6) The Overlapping Sets Formula – A third way to solve Overlapping Sets problems is with the "Overlapping Sets Formula".

• As we've discussed, Venn Diagrams allow you to visualize the intersection of sets, but can be awkward to use. The Overlapping Sets Table is smart and effective, but can take time to learn.

➤ The formula is the EASIEST of the three strategies, but also the most limited. In general, it's only helpful when a question does NOT involve "ONLY groups".

• By "only groups", we mean the group of people or objects that are in "Group *A* but not Group *B*" or "Group *B* but not Group *A*".

• In other words, a problem that mentions a group of people who "are in one group but not another", or are "only in one particular group", would NOT be a great candidate for the Overlapping Sets Formula.

➤ There are several ways to express the formula. The version that we prefer is as follows:

$$\boxed{\textbf{Group } A + \textbf{Group } B + \textbf{Neither} - \textbf{Both} = \textbf{Total}}$$

• Imagine a school of 70 students, in which 30 study French, 50 study Spanish, and 10 study neither. To determine the number of the students who study both French and Spanish, we simply need to plug this information into the formula as follows:

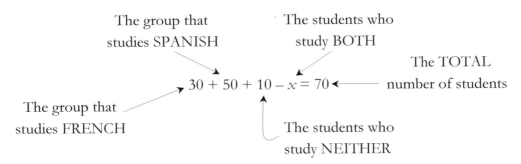

• Thus, 20 students study both languages, since:

$$30 + 50 + 10 - x = 70$$
$$90 - x = 70$$
$$x = 20$$

➤ Group *A* + Group *B* represents the sum of everyone who belongs to either of the two groups.

• That sum double-counts the members who do BOTH. That's why we subtract the members in both groups from Group *A* + Group *B*.

• To ensure that you've got the hang of the Overlapping Sets Formula, let's take a look at another example:

Jefferson High School has 80 students. 50 students study Biology and 25 students study both Biology and Chemistry. If 10 students study neither Biology nor Chemistry, how many students study Chemistry?

(A) 25   (B) 30   (C) 35   (D) 45   (E) 45

Answer: E. According to the problem, Jefferson has a total of 80 students, of whom 50 study Biology, 25 study Biology and Chemistry, and 10 study neither. Plugging this information into the Overlapping Sets Formula proves that 45 students study Chemistry, as:

$$Biology + Chemistry + Neither - Both = Total$$

$$50 + x + 10 - 25 = 80$$
$$60 + x = 105$$
$$x = 45$$

➤ The Overlapping Sets Formula is NOT something you NEED to commit to memory.

• It is simply a SHORTCUT that can come in handy with relatively simple problems. So if you're looking to master every possible advantage, or are having a hard time using the Overlapping Sets Table, this formula may be worth your time.

• Otherwise, you're better off focusing on more critical material. Remember, the table can solve any problem the formula can solve, and in most cases is the faster, more effective strategy.

Rare or Advanced Concepts

(7) Algebraic Relationships – In more difficult overlapping sets problems, you may come across two groups linked together through an algebraic relationship.

- For example, you might be told that "some people prefer brand *B*, but 10% still use brand *A*" or that "some students study French, of whom 30% do not study Spanish."

  ➤ Because such relationships do NOT contain numbers, you must represent them with VARIABLES.

- In other words, if "some people prefer brand *B*, but 10% of those people still use brand *A*", the people who **prefer** $B = x$, but the people who **prefer** B **but use** $A = 0.1x$.

- To get a sense of how this might affect an overlapping sets problem, consider the following:

40% of the students in a biology course passed a quiz. Of those students who failed the quiz, 16 studied and 32 did not study. How many students passed the quiz?

(A) 12   (B) 16   (C) 20   (D) 24   (E) 32

Answer: E. The biology course has two groups of students: those **who passed the quiz** and **those who studied**. Thus, every student in the course either (1) passed the quiz or failed, (2) studied or did not study.

	Pass	Fail	Total
Study		16	
No Study		32	
Total	0.4*x*	48	*x*

The problem states that of the students who **failed the quiz**, 16 studied and 32 did not. The problem also states that "40% of the students in the course **passed the quiz**."

Because the exact number of students in the course is **unknown**, we can let the **total group** = *x* and the **pass group** = 0.4*x*, as shown above. We can also use the bottom row of the table to determine that *x* = 80, as:

$$0.4x + 48 = x$$
$$48 = 0.6x$$
$$\frac{48}{0.6} = \frac{480}{6} = 80 = x$$

If *x* = 80, then the number of students who **passed the quiz** must be 32, since 0.4*x* equals 0.4(80) = 4(8) = 32.

> ➤ Beware. The phrasing of advanced overlapping set questions is often intentionally CONVOLUTED.

- It is worth your time to interpret the phrasing of such problems CAREFULLY. The devil's often in the details, so a little extra caution can be the difference between wrong and right.

- Consider the following:

A recent survey of 100 children found that 20 percent eat their vegetables but don't do their homework and that 80 percent who do their homework eat their vegetables. If 40 percent of the children surveyed eat their vegetables, how many do not eat their vegetables but do their homework?

(A) 4   (B) 5   (C) 7   (D) 8   (E) 9

Answer. B. The survey has two groups of children: **those who eat their vegetables** and **those who do their homework**. Therefore, every child in the survey either (1) eats vegetables or doesn't, (2) does homework or doesn't.

The problem states that of the 100 children surveyed, "20% eat their vegetables but don't do their homework." The problem also states that "80% of the children who do their homework eat their vegetables." As such, you may want to assign an 80 to the intersection of "Veggies" and "HW", as follows:

$$\boxed{\text{WRONG}}$$

	Veg.	No Veg.	Total
HW	80	⬭	
No HW	20		
Total			100

Unfortunately, doing so would be a mistake. The problem tells us that 80% of the children who do their homework eat their vegetables. **This does not mean that 80% of the children eat their veggies and do their homework.** On the contrary, it means that 80% of the children who do homework – a group whose quantity is unknown – eat their veggies.

Because we do not know the exact number of children who do their homework, we must let the **children who do their homework** = x. Likewise, if 80% of the children who do their homework eat their vegetables, we can let the children **who do their homework and eat their vegetables** = $0.8x$.

Given that 20% of the children surveyed eat their vegetables but don't do their homework and that 40% eat their vegetables, our table is therefore correctly completed as follows:

$$\boxed{\text{CORRECT}}$$

	Veg.	No Veg.	Total
HW	$0.8x$	$0.2x$	
No HW	20		
Total	40	60	100

According to the "Veggie" column, $0.8x + 20 = 40$. From this, we know that $x = 25$, since:

$$0.8x + 20 = 40$$
$$0.8x = 20$$
$$x = \frac{20}{0.8} = \frac{200}{8} = \frac{2(100)}{2(4)} = 25$$

If $x = 25$, then the number of children surveyed who **do not eat their vegetables but do their homework** must be 5, since our table contains a $0.2x$ at the intersection of "veggies" and "homework". Thus:

$$0.2x = 0.2(25) = 2(2.5) = 5$$

(8) Hidden Information – Overlapping Sets questions sometimes hide by implying it rather than stating it directly.

• Such questions are deceptively difficult, since they're designed to make you ignore critical information.

➤ To protect yourself, watch out for groups that are MUTUALLY EXCLUSIVE or naturally ALL-INCLUSIVE.

• Consider the following:

Company *A* has 21 board members, some of whom belong to the board of company *B*, which has 11 members. At a joint meeting of the boards, all 25 members were present.

Quantity A   **Quantity B**

The number of staff members   7
who belong to both companies

Answer: C. The problem above has two groups of board members: **those in company *A*** and **those in company *B***. Thus, every board member is either: (1) in *A* or not in *A*, (2) in *B* or not in *B*.

The problem states that company *A* has 21 board members and that company *B* has 11 board members. The problem also states that "at a joint meeting of the boards, all 25 members were present." From this, we know that the 25 board members must represent the **total number** of members of the combined boards.

We also know, however, that **ZERO people at the meeting belonged to neither board.** After all, if the meeting was a "joint meeting of the boards", everyone who attended the meeting must have belonged to one of the two companies!

	A	No *A*	Total
B	7	4	11
No B	14	0	14
Total	21	4	25

As such, there must be 7 members who belong to **both boards**, since our table contains a 7 at the intersection of "*A*" and "*B*".

Therefore, the two quantities are equal. Alternatively, we could also have used the Overlapping Set Formula, as follows:

$$\text{Group } A + \text{Group } B + \text{Neither} - \text{Both} = \text{Total}$$

$$21 + 11 + 0 - x = 25$$
$$32 - x = 25$$
$$x = 7$$

- A second problem for you:

At restaurant R, 15 percent of the full-time employees are chefs and 60 percent are waiters. If restaurant R has 5 other full-time employees, how many full-time employees at restaurant R are not chefs?

(A) 9   (B) 11   (C) 17   (D) 23   (E) 29

Answer. C. This problem mentions two types of full-time employees at restaurant R: **those who are chefs** and **those who are waiters**. Thus, every full-time employee is either (1) a chef or not a chef, (2) a waiter or not a waiter.

Because this percent problem contains actual quantities, we CANNOT let the number of employees = 100. Further, **full-time chefs cannot be full-time waiters**, so we can assign a 0 to the intersection of "chef" and "waiter".

The problem states that "15 percent of the full-time employees are chefs" and that "60 percent (of the full-time employees) are waiters".

	Chef	No Chef	Total
Waiter	0	$0.6x$	$0.6x$
No Waiter	$0.15x$	5	$0.4x$
Total	$0.15x$	$0.85x$	x

Because we don't know the number of full-time employees, we can let **full-time employees** = x, **full-time chefs** = $0.15x$, and **full-time waiters** = $0.6x$.

Plugging the rest of the provided information into an Overlapping Sets Table reveals that $0.15x + 5 = 0.4x$. Thus, $x = 20$, since:

$$0.15x + 5 = 0.4x$$
$$5 = 0.25x$$
$$\frac{5}{0.25} = \frac{500}{25} = \frac{5(100)}{25} = 5(4) = 20$$

If $x = 20$, then the number of full-time employees at restaurant R who are not chefs must be 17, since $0.85x$ of the full-time employees are not chefs, and $0.85(20) = 8.5(2) = 17$.

(9) Maximization Problems – Some of the most difficult Overlapping Sets questions involve a category whose membership falls within a range of possibilities.

• We call them "maximization problems", since to solve them you typically need to establish some possible maximum, as well as some possible minimum.

➢ Such problems generally contain phrases such as "at least", "no less than", "no more than", "maximum", "minimum", or "could be".

• To solve them, you usually need to make TWO Overlapping Sets Tables. In the first, consider the MAXIMUM number of possibilities. In the second, consider the MINIMUM.

• Combined, the two scenarios will establish a range of options. Consider the following:

A language department has 40 students. 10 of the students study Hittite and 5 study Sanskrit. If no more than 3 study both Hittite and Sanskrit, then the number of students that study neither language could be which of the following?

Select all such numbers.

A 23　**B** 25　**C** 27　**D** 29　**E** 31

Answer: B and C. The department has two groups of students: **those who study Hittite** and **those who study Sanskrit**. Thus, every student either (1) studies Hittite or does not, (2) studies Sanskrit or does not.

The problem states that the department has a total of 40 students, of which 10 study Hittite and 5 study Sanskrit. The problem also states that "**no more** than 3 students study both Hittite and Sanskrit", indicating that **as many as three** students and **as few as zero** students may study both languages.

To determine the range of students who may study neither language, we need to consider both scenarios.

MAXIMUM Scenario: 3 students study both languages.

	Hittite	No Hitt.	Total
Sanskrit	3	2	5
No Sanskrit	7	28	35
Total	10	30	40

MINIMUM Scenario: 0 students study both languages.

	Hittite	No Hitt.	Total
Sanskrit	0	5	5
No Sanskrit	10	25	35
Total	10	30	40

According to the maximum scenario, 28 students study both languages. According to the minimum scenario, 25 students study both languages. Thus, the number of students who study neither language can range from 25 to 28.

> ➤ Maximization problems sometimes have UNSTATED restrictions that constrain a possible maximum or minimum.

• Fortunately, the Overlapping Sets Table can help you spot those restrictions. Just remember that the rows and columns of your table CANNOT EXCEED their TOTALS.

• To get a sense of what we mean by this, consider the following:

Of the 180 cars in lot *L*, 110 have air-conditioning and 130 have automatic transmissions. If at least 20 of the cars have neither air-conditioning nor automatic transmissions, then the number of cars in lot *L* that have both air-conditioning and automatic transmissions could equal which of the following?

Select <u>all</u> such numbers.

$\boxed{\text{A}}$ 70 $\boxed{\text{B}}$ 80 $\boxed{\text{C}}$ 90 $\boxed{\text{D}}$ 110 $\boxed{\text{E}}$ 130

Answer: B, C, and D. Lot *L* has two groups of cars: **those that have air-conditioning** and **those that have automatic transmissions**. Thus, every car either (1) has air-conditioning or does not, (2) has an automatic transmission or does not.

The problem states that lot *L* has 180 cars, of which 110 have air-conditioning and 130 have automatic transmissions. The problem also states that "**at least 20** cars have neither air-conditioning nor automatic transmissions", indicating that **as few as 20** and **as many as all** the cars CAN lack both conveniences.

To determine the range of cars that have both air and automatic transmissions, we need to consider BOTH scenarios.

MINIMUM Scenario: 20 cars have neither air-conditioning nor automatic transmissions.

	Air	No Air	Total
Trans	80	50	130
No Trans	30	20	50
Total	110	70	180

MAXIMUM Scenario: 180 cars have neither air-conditioning nor automatic transmissions.

	Air	No Air	Total
Trans			130
No Trans		180 ??	50
Total	110	**70**	180

The NEITHER category cannot exceed this amount

The NEITHER category cannot exceed this amount either

We know that it is impossible for all the cars to have neither air-conditioning nor automatic transmissions since the problem tell us that 110 have air-conditioning and 130 have automatic transmissions.

However, if we plug a 180 into the **neither portion** of our table, we quickly see that the number of cars that have neither air-conditioning nor automatic transmissions **cannot be larger than 50**, as any number larger than 50 would exceed the number to the RIGHT of the neither slot.

Since the maximum number of cars that can have neither air-conditioning nor automatic transmissions is 50, our **actual Maximum Scenario** is as follows:

	Air	No Air	Total
Trans	110	20	130
No Trans	0	**50**	50
Total	110	70	180

According to the minimum scenario, 80 cars have air-conditioning and automatic transmissions. According to the maximum scenario, 110 cars have both features. Thus, the number of cars with both air-conditioning and automatic transmissions can range from 80 to 110.

(10) Three-Part Overlapping Sets – Problems involving three overlapping sets are extremely rare for the GRE.

• They can also be fairly intimidating. Let's take a look at an example:

School *S* has 161 students, all of whom study math in at least one of three semesters. 77 students study math in the fall, 83 in the winter, and 80 in the spring. If 39 students study math in exactly two semesters, how many study math in all three?

(A) 13   (B) 17   (C) 19   (D) 20   (E) 21

➢ Unfortunately, we CANNOT use an Overlapping Sets Table to solve such a problem, since it would need to have three-dimensions in order to represent all three groups.

• A Venn Diagram wouldn't be of much help either, since there would be no place to represent the 39 students.

• Fortunately, problems like this can be solved quite easily through a simple extension of the Overlapping Sets Formula.

➢ As with the formula for two sets, there are several ways to express the formula for three sets.

• The version that we prefer is as follows:

Groups $(A + B + C)$ + None – "Exactly Two" – $(2 \times$ "All Three"$)$ = Total

• At first glance, this may seem rather complicated, but it's really a trivial expansion of the two-set formula. Groups $(A + B + C)$ represent the sum of all the students who study math in one or more semesters.

• Since 39 students study math in "EXACTLY TWO" semesters, we've DOUBLE-COUNTED 39 students and so must subtract 39 from the sum of the groups.

➢ Similarly, some group of students study math in "ALL THREE" semesters, so we've also TRIPLE-COUNTED some students.

• Thus, we must subtract that unknown number TWICE from the sum of the groups.

• In this problem, we've been told that 77 students study math in the fall, 83 in the winter, 80 in the spring. The phrase "in at least one of three semesters" tells us that none of the 161 students study math in NONE of the three semesters.

- Therefore, to determine how many students study math in ALL THREE semesters, we simply need to plug this information into the formula as follows:

The students who study in
EXACTLY TWO semesters

The students who study in
ALL THREE semesters is unknown

$$(77 + 82 + 83) + 0 - 39 - 2x = 161 \longleftarrow \text{The TOTAL students}$$

The groups that study in
FALL, WINTER, or SPRING

The students who study
in NONE of the semesters

- Thus, the correct answer is (D), since 20 students study math in all three semesters:

$$(77 + 83 + 80) + 0 - 39 - 2x = 161$$
$$240 - 2x = 200$$
$$2x = 40$$
$$x = 20$$

➢ To ensure that you've got the hang of the formula for three overlapping sets, let's take a look at another example:

72 students at Adams High School study Physics or Calculus or German. Exactly 41 study Physics, 29 study Calculus, and 35 study German. If 14 students study all three subjects, how many students study exactly two of the subjects?

(A) 3 (B) 5 (C) 6 (D) 8 (E) 9

Answer. B. According to the problem, Adams has 72 students, of whom 41 study Physics, 29 study Calculus, and 35 study German. Of the 72 total students, everyone studies at least one of the subjects, so no one studies NONE of them, and 14 study all three.

Plugging this information into the formula for three-part overlapping sets proves that 5 students study exactly two of the subjects, since:

$$\text{Groups } (A + B + C) + \text{None} - \text{"Exactly Two"} - (2 \times \text{"All Three"}) = \text{Total}$$

$$(41 + 29 + 35) + 0 - x - 2(14) = 72$$
$$105 - x - 28 = 72$$
$$105 - x = 100$$
$$x = 5$$

(11) Intersections & Unions – On very rare occasions, Overlapping Sets questions feature the symbol ∩ or the symbol ∪.

- These symbols refer to the intersection and union of sets.

  ➢ The INTERSECTION of two sets is the set of elements that are in BOTH sets, and is denoted by the symbol ∩.

- In the diagram below, the grey region that is a part of set *A* and set *B* can be referred to as *A* ∩ *B*, since it is the intersection of the two sets:

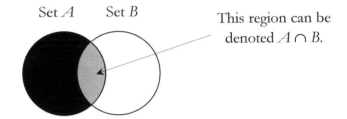

This region can be denoted *A* ∩ *B*.

  ➢ Conversely, the UNION of two sets is the set of elements that are ONLY in ONE of the two sets <u>or</u> in BOTH sets, and is denoted by the symbol ∪.

- In the diagram below, the three colored regions can be referred to as *X* ∪ *Y*, since together they represent every element that's only in set *X*, only in set *Y*, or in both sets:

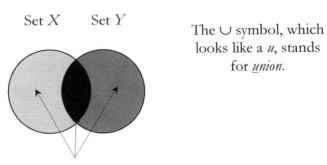

The ∪ symbol, which looks like a *u*, stands for <u>*union*</u>.

These 3 regions are the **union** of sets *X* and *Y* and can be denoted *X* ∪ *Y*.

  ➢ To get a sense of how the GRE might test your understanding of intersections and unions, let's work through a practice problem together.

- Consider the following:

One measurement is to be selected at random from a study, in which 1/3 of the measurements are in set A, 2/5 of the measurements are in set B, and 1/4 of the measurements are in both sets.

Quantity A	**Quantity B**
The probability of selecting a measurement in $A \cup B$	0.5

Answer: B. This study has two groups of measurements: **those in set A** and **those in set B**. Thus, every measurement is (1) either in set A or not in set A; (2) either in set B or not in set B.

➤ Because this problem has fractions but NO numbers, we can let the **number of measurements** = 60, which is the product of the problem's denominators: $3 \times 5 \times 4$.

• The problem states that 1/3 of the measurements are in set A, 2/5 are in set B, and 1/4 are in both sets.

• Hence, we can say that 20 measurements are **in set A**, since 1/3 of 60 = 20; 24 measurements are **in set B**, since 2/5 of 60 = 24; and 15 measurements are **in both sets**, since 1/4 of 60 = 15.

➤ Completing an Overlapping Sets table tells us that 5 measurements are **in set A but not set B** and that 9 measurements are **in set B but not set A**:

	A	No A	Total
B	15	9	24
No B	5	31	36
Total	20	40	60

In an overlapping sets table, these 3 slots represent the **union** of the two sets.

• The union of two sets is the set of elements that are ONLY in ONE of the two sets <u>or</u> in BOTH sets.

• Thus, the number of measurements in $A \cup B$ is 5 + 9 + 15 = 29, since 5 measurements are in set A but not set B, 9 are in set B but not set A, and 15 are in both sets. If 29 of the 60 measurements belong to $A \cup B$, then the correct answer must be (B), since Quantity A equals 29/60, which is slightly less than 30/60, or 0.5.

Practice Questions

(12) Problem Sets – The following questions have been arranged into three groups: fundamental, intermediate, and rare or advanced.

• Whether you're aiming for a perfect score or a score closer to average, mastery of the concepts in the FUNDAMENTAL questions is absolutely essential.

> ➢ As you might expect, the INTERMEDIATE questions are more difficult but are essential for test-takers who need an above-average score or higher.

• Finally, the RARE or ADVANCED questions test concepts that are very sophisticated or seldom encountered on the GRE. Mastery of such questions is required only if you need a math score above the 90th percentile.

• As always, if you find yourself confused, bogged down with busy work, or stuck, don't be afraid to fall back on your "Plan B" strategies!

Fundamental

1. The campus of college X is home to 70 squirrels. 55 of the squirrels are grey and 10 of the squirrels do not have fluffy tails. If 8 of these squirrels are not grey and do have fluffy tails, how many squirrels are grey but do not have fluffy tails?

    (A) 3   (B) 5   (C) 8   (D) 15   (E) 18

Of the 480 members in a club of men and women, 320 are women and 1/2 of the female and 3/4 of the male participants do not have professional degrees.

Quantity A	Quantity B

2. The fraction of members in the club without a degree $\dfrac{5}{9}$

3. 60% of the world's monkeys are depressed and 10% have jobs as butlers. If the world's monkey population is down to 600 monkeys, and 30 monkeys are depressed butlers, how many are neither depressed nor butlers?

    (A) 120   (B) 150   (C) 180   (D) 210   (E) 240

4.   15% of the students at Lincoln High School are gifted and 55% are female. If 10% of the students are both gifted and female, what percent is neither gifted nor female?

(A) 20%   (B) 30%   (C) 35%   (D) 40%   (E) 50%

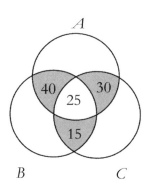

In the diagram above, 120 objects belong to set *A*, 100 belong to set *B*, and 150 belong to set *C*.

Quantity A	Quantity B
5.   The number of objects in exactly one set | 100 |

Intermediate

Last year, 54 houses out of a group of 63 were renovated or sold, or both. 47 of these houses were renovated and 41 were sold.

Quantity A	Quantity B
6.   The number of houses that were renovated but not sold | The number of houses that were not renovated |

7.   The total number of books published by publishers *A* and *B* is 830. The number of books published by *A* is 610 and the number of books published by *B* is 520. Which of the following statements must be true?

Select <u>all</u> such statements.

A   More than half of the books published by *A* are also published by *B*.
B   More than half of the books published by *B* are also published by *A*.
C   No books are published by both *A* and *B*.

If A and B are sets of marbles, $A \ominus B$ denotes the set of marbles that belong to set A or set B, but not both. A consists of 17 marbles, B consists of 21 marbles, and 9 of the marbles are in both A and B.

	Quantity A	Quantity B
8.	The total number of marbles in sets A and B combined	$A \ominus B$

9. In school S, 76 percent of the students are male and 19 percent of the students are male juniors. What percent of the male students in school S are not juniors?

$$\boxed{}$$

10. In a certain lot, 3/4 of the cars are black, including 2/3 of the sedans. If 3/5 of the cars are sedans, what percent of the cars that are not black are sedans?

(A) 50 (B) 60 (C) 65 (D) 70 (E) 80

Rare or Advanced

A recent poll of 400 adults found that 5 percent neither wash their hands nor brush their teeth before going to bed, 15 percent only wash their hands, and for every adult that does both, 3 only brushed their teeth.

	Quantity A	Quantity B
11.	The number of adults surveyed that do not wash their hands before bed	280

12. A certain choir has an equal number of male and female members. If 1/3 of the members are tenors and 2/3 of those who are not tenors are female, what portion of the choir is comprised of male tenors?

(A) $\frac{1}{18}$ (B) $\frac{1}{9}$ (C) $\frac{1}{6}$ (D) $\frac{2}{9}$ (E) $\frac{5}{18}$

13. At a local high school, 20 percent of the students are juniors and 70 percent are not sophomores. Approximately what percentage of those students who are not sophomores are juniors?

    (A) 24% (B) 28% (C) 31% (D) 33% (E) 34%

	Love	Hate	Indifferent
Chocolate	80	40	80
Vanilla	60	70	70

The table above shows the results of a recent poll in which 200 teenagers were asked whether they "loved", "hated", or were "indifferent" to two flavors of ice cream. The number of teenagers who did not respond "love" for either flavor was 80.

Quantity A	Quantity B

14. The number of teenagers who responded "love" for both flavors

    20

15. At a certain college, there are 242 sophomores, of whom 148 are taking an economics course and 127 are taking a literature course. What is the greatest possible number of sophomores that could be taking both an economics course and a literature course?

16. Of 200 subjects who tested a certain drug, 40 percent experienced nausea, 30 percent experienced dizziness, and 60 percent dry skin. If all of the subjects experienced at least one of these effects and 5 percent experienced exactly two of these effects, how many experienced only one of these effects?

    (A) 145 (B) 150 (C) 165 (D) 170 (E) 185

At school S, 1/4 of all students study Physics, 30 more than 1/2 of all students study science, and 1/3 of those studying science study Physics.

Quantity A	Quantity B

17. The number of students studying Physics

    30

(13) Solutions – Video solutions for each of the previous questions can be found on our website at **www.sherpaprep.com/videos**.

- BOOKMARK this address for future visits!

  ➢ To view the videos, you'll need the LOGIN and PASSWORD that you created upon registering your copy of Word Problems.

- If you have yet to register your book yet, please go to **www.sherpaprep.com/activate** and enter your email address, last name, and shipping address.

- Be sure to provide the SAME last name and shipping address that you used to purchase your copy of Master Key to the GRE or to enroll in your GRE course with Sherpa Prep!

  ➢ When checking your answers, we encourage you to watch the solution for any problem that you answered INCORRECTLY

- The same goes for any problem that took you MORE than TWO MINUTES to solve.

- After digesting the explanation, REVISIT your mistake a couple of days later to ensure that the problem no longer poses issues to you.

  ➢ If you struggle to solve the problem a SECOND time, add it to your "LOG of ERRORS" and redo it every few weeks.

- Solving tricky questions MORE THAN ONCE is the best way to learn from your mistakes and to avoid similar difficulties on your actual exam.

Fundamental	Intermediate	Rare or Advanced
1. A	6. B	11. B
2. A	7. B	12. E
3. D	8. A	13. B
4. D	9. 75	14. C
5. A	10. E	15. 127
		16. C
		17. C

Sherpa Prep

Master Key to the GRE

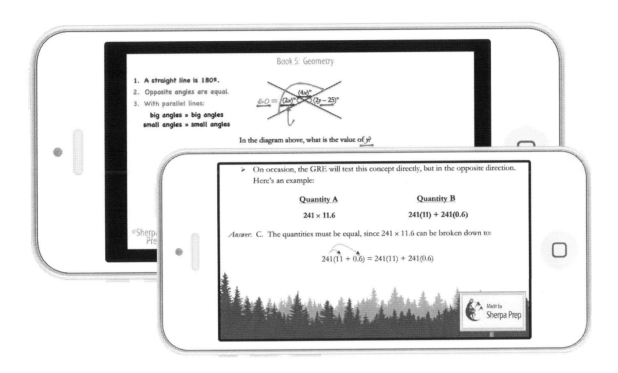

Notes

—

Made in the USA
Middletown, DE
23 July 2017